Housing Regeneration

Written from an 'in-house' perspective in response to the UK Government Housing White Paper released in February 2017, *Housing Regeneration: A Plan for Implementation* presents sustainable solutions to Britain's housing crisis and will be a useful practical guide for anyone involved in the process of regeneration. Taking as its starting point an idea for a housing regeneration scheme, it provides an overview of each of the issues to be considered and the options for addressing them. In clear and concise language, it explains the issues and work involved in a regeneration scheme, answering questions such as who is involved, how is it paid for, what options are available and, importantly, what are the risks. It will appeal to lawyers, councillors, town planners, surveyors, chief officers, finance officers, procurement officers, project managers and students, amongst others.

V. Charles Ward is a solicitor and a Legal Associate of the Royal Town Planning Institute. His professional background spans private practice, industry, local government and urban regeneration projects. Since 2013 he has been working as a property lawyer with HB Public Law, a shared legal service acting for several local authorities. Other books by Charles Ward include *Residential Leaseholders' Handbook*, published in 2006.

Housing Regeneration
A Plan for Implementation

V. Charles Ward

LONDON AND NEW YORK

First published 2018
by Routledge
2 Park Square, Milton Park, Abingdon, Oxon OX14 4RN

and by Routledge
711 Third Avenue, New York, NY 10017

Routledge is an imprint of the Taylor & Francis Group, an informa business

© 2018 V. Charles Ward

The right of V. Charles Ward to be identified as author of this work has been asserted by him in accordance with sections 77 and 78 of the Copyright, Designs and Patents Act 1988.

All rights reserved. No part of this book may be reprinted or reproduced or utilised in any form or by any electronic, mechanical, or other means, now known or hereafter invented, including photocopying and recording, or in any information storage or retrieval system, without permission in writing from the publishers.

Trademark notice: Product or corporate names may be trademarks or registered trademarks, and are used only for identification and explanation without intent to infringe.

British Library Cataloguing-in-Publication Data
A catalogue record for this book is available from the British Library

Library of Congress Cataloging-in-Publication Data
Names: Ward, Charles, author.
Title: Housing regeneration : a plan for implementation / V. Charles Ward.
Description: Abingdon, Oxon [UK] ; New York, NY : Routledge, [2018] | Includes bibliographical references and index.
Identifiers: LCCN 2017055440 | ISBN 9780815370246 (hardback) | ISBN 9781351249942 (ebook)
Subjects: LCSH: Public housing—Law and legislation—Great Britain. | Housing policy—Great Britain. | City planning and redevelopment law—Great Britain. | Urban renewal—Great Britain.
Classification: LCC KD1179 .W35 2018 | DDC 344.41/063635—dc23
LC record available at https://lccn.loc.gov/2017055440

ISBN: 978-0-815-37024-6 (hbk)
ISBN: 978-1-351-24994-2 (ebk)

Typeset in Times New Roman
by Apex CoVantage, LLC

Contents

Table of statutes vi
Table of statutory instruments and circulars viii
Table of cases x
Table of other source material xi

Introduction 1

1 The route map 9

2 Information gathering 15

3 Statutory constraints 23

4 Development options 40

5 Compulsory purchase 48

6 Other statutory tools 63

7 Constitutional and procurement issues 79

8 Funding considerations and options 86

9 Documenting the project 99

10 Local authority companies 108

Index 122

Table of statutes

Academies Act 2010	37
Acquisition of Land Act 1981	48
Allotments Act 1925	37
Audit Commission Act 1998	112
Charities Act 2011	38
Commons Act 2006	38
Commons Registration Act 1965	38
Companies Act 2006	119–20
Co-operative and Community Benefit Societies Act 2014	118
General Vesting Declaration Act 1981	48
Green Belt (London and Home Counties) Act 1938	39
Highways Act 1980	76–7
Housing Act 1957	5
Housing Act 1980	4
Housing Act 1985	23–4, 40
Housing Act 1988	4
Housing Act 1996	4
Land Compensation Act 1961	48, 54
Land Compensation Act 1973	48, 54
Law of Property Act 1925	63–4
Law of Property (Miscellaneous Provisions) Act 1989	49
Limited Liability Partnership Act 2000	115
Local Authorities (Land) Act 1963	47
Local Democracy Economic Development and Construction Act 2009	117
Local Government (Contracts) Act 1997	13
Local Government (Miscellaneous Provisions) Act 1976	49
Local Government Act 1972	33–6, 114
Local Government Act 1988	25–9
Local Government Act 2000	115
Local Government Act 2003	92–3, 115–16

Table of statutes vii

Local Government and Housing Act 1989	100–01, 110
Localism Act 2011	116–7
Open Spaces Act 1906	37–8
Public Health Act 1875	37–8
Rent Act 1977	2–3
School Standards and Framework Act 1998	17
Town and Country Planning Act 1990	30–3, 63

Table of statutory instruments and circulars

Academies General Disposal and Appropriation Consent (No 2) 2012	37
Circular 6/93: Local Government Act 1972 general disposal consent (England) 2003: disposal of land for less than the best consideration that can reasonably be obtained.	36–7
Community Infrastructure Levy Regulations 2010	90–1
Compulsory Purchase (Inquiries Procedure) Rules 2007	52
Compulsory Purchase Process and the Crichel Down Rules 2015	48
Equality Act 2010	58
European Convention on Human Rights	58
General Block Exemption Regulation	98
General Consent under Section 25 of the Local Government Act 1988 for the disposal of land to registered providers of social housing 2010	26–9
General Consent under Section 25 of the Local Government Act 1988 for the disposal of Housing Revenue Account Land 2014	29
General Housing Consents 2013	24–5
HMRC Guidance 'Stamp Duty Land Tax: Relief for Land or Property Transactions (2014)	87–8
Housing and Planning Act 2016	64–66
Local Authorities (Capital Financing and Accounting) (England) Regulations 2003	93
Local Authorities (Companies) Order 1995	112–13
Local Authorities (Indemnities for Members and Officers) Order 2004	121
Local Government (Best Value Authorities) (Power to Trade) (England) Order 2009	115–16
Public Contracts Regulations 2015	82–84

Regulatory Reform (Housing Assistance) (England and Wales)
　Order 2002　60–1
School Playing Fields General Disposal and Change of
　use Consent (No 5) 2014　37
State Aid: The Basics Guide (2015)　96
VAT Notice 742: Land and Property (2012)　89
VAT Notice 749: Local Authorities and Similar Bodies (2016)　89–90

Table of cases

Associated Provincial Picture Houses v Wednesbury Corporation [1948] 1 KB 223 — 4
Credit Suisse v Allerdale Borough Council [1995] 1 Lloyd's Rep 215 — 109–10
Credit Suisse v Waltham Forest LBC (1994) Times, 2 November — 109–10
Jelson Ltd v Derby City Council [2000] JPL 203 — 101
Milebush Properties Ltd v Tameside MBC and Hillingdon LBC [2010] EWHC 1022 and [2011] EWCA Civ 270 — 101–02
R (ex parte Risk Management Partners) v Brent LBC [2008] EWHC 692 (Admin) — 117
Street v Mountford [1985] WLR 877 — 3

Table of other source material

Agar Grove Estate	9–10, 56–8
Briars, Copshall Close and Aylets Field	67–9
Civitas Report: The Future of Private Renting (January 2015)	2–3
Ebury Bridge Estate	58
Gateshead Regeneration LLP	46
Greater London Assembly Housing Committee Paper, 'Right to Build. What's stopping councils from building more housing' (October 2013)	6
Grenfell Tower	13–14
Hackney Council's multi-site regeneration programme	10–11
HCA Development Partner Panel 3	84
House of Commons Briefing Paper 'Local Government in England: Capital Finance' (2016)	93–4
House of Commons Briefing Paper 'The General Power of Competence' (2016)	117–18
Housing White Paper: Fixing our Broken Housing Market (2017)	1–3
Loddon Homes	
London Borough of Camden (Part of Agar Grove Estate) Compulsory Purchase Order 2015	56–8
Meadway Regeneration	80–2
Sir Michael Latham's Report 'Contracting the Team' 1994	107
Sussex Weald Homes Limited	45
Wealden Housing and Regeneration Company	42–5

Introduction

Almost as the first words of this book were being written, Theresa May's Conservative Government published its February 2017 Housing White Paper: 'Fixing Our Broken Housing Market'.

The Paper paints a gloomy picture of a Britain in which home ownership has become a distant dream for millions of young, hard-working people. It is right about that. Rocketing house prices have made home ownership unaffordable for first-time buyers.

Even the private rented market is fast becoming unaffordable. Without massive financial subsidy, in the form of Housing Benefit, many households on modest income would not even be able to afford a place to live. But public resources are finite. Housing Benefit cannot be an open cheque book, even though it is demand-led. Its budget has to compete with other calls on public finance.

As the White Paper points out, it is about supply and demand. There are not enough new homes being built. England needs up to 275,000 new homes each year just to keep up with population growth and to tackle years of under supply. Against this there has only been an average 160,000 new homes built each year since the 1970s.

The White Paper is also right in its assertion that local authorities have a role to play in getting new houses built and in a way which is affordable. It is local authorities which control many of the statutory gateways to new development, including our system of town and country planning. It is local authorities who are vast landowners in their own right. As paragraph 2.43 of the White Paper states:

> *Compulsory Purchase Law gives local authorities extensive powers to assemble land for development. Through the Housing and Planning Act 2016 and the Neighbourhood Planning Bill currently in Parliament we are reforming compulsory purchase to make the process clearer, fairer and faster, while retaining proper protections for landowners. Local*

2 Introduction

authorities should now think about how they can use these powers to promote development, which is particularly important in areas of high housing need.

It adds in paragraph 2.44, '*We propose to encourage more active use of compulsory purchase powers to promote development on stalled sites for housing.*'

Unfortunately, in spite of the good intentions, the White Paper has not addressed the obstacles which local authorities face in getting sufficient new social housing built out to meet their statutory responsibilities. Instead it threatens to make those obstacles worse. Take paragraph 3.29 of the White Paper:

Increasingly and across the country local authorities are using innovative models to get homes built in their area. There are a number of good examples of Local Development Corporations, local housing companies and/or joint venture models building mixed sites, which include new market housing for sale or private rent, as well as affordable housing. We welcome innovations like these, and want more local authorities to get building. To that end we will seek to address the issues that hold them back. However, we want to see tenants that local authorities place in new affordable properties offered equivalent terms to those in council housing, including a right to buy their home.

Many Government policies which seemed right in the 1980s are today inhibiting local authority new-build. It means that any local council wishing to build new affordable housing – whether alone or more commonly through a private-sector partner – must first circumvent a maze of legislative traps. Back in the 1980s the housing landscape was different.

When the modern Housing Benefit regime was first introduced in the early 1980s, there was almost no private-rented market. According to figures contained in the January 2015 Civitas Report 'The Future of Private Renting', in 1918 76% of households (in England and Wales) rented privately, compared to a low point of 9% in 1991. However, of that 9%, many occupiers would have been long-term sitting tenants whose rights to occupy were already protected under the 1977 Rent Act. Once that tenant died or moved out, a wise landlord might take the opportunity to sell the property with vacant possession. It would not be re-let.

Safe legal advice to anyone thinking of renting out their home was 'don't'. Letting was high risk. Once a residential tenant was installed, and so long as they paid their rent, they were potentially there for life. To make matters worse, whatever rent the prospective landlord and prospective tenant

Introduction 3

might agree at the outset, the tenant could later apply to a Rent Assessment Committee or Tribunal to get it reduced. Some private landlords dreamed up innovative schemes to get around lifetime security and rent controls. These included non-exclusive possession licences, where the landlord was not technically a landlord at all and the tenant was not technically a tenant. So, the 1977 Rent Act could not apply. However, the House of Lords had no hesitation in striking down such sham arrangements in the case of *Street v Mountford* [1985] WLR 877, when it ruled that, in the absence of exceptional circumstances, the grant of exclusive possession of accommodation to someone in return for a rent constituted a tenancy to which the Rent Act applied, whatever the piece of paper might say.

The new Thatcher Government had in 1980 legislated to create a new form of Protected Shorthold Tenancy, which would give landlords the right to let residential properties for fixed terms of between one and five years and with the ability regain possession of their properties after the terms had ended. During the term of the protected shorthold, the tenant would enjoy all the rights of a Rent Act regulated tenancy. But there were strict procedures for setting it up, which included service of a 'Section 53 Notice' on the tenant before the tenancy agreement was signed. Getting it wrong meant that the tenancy would default to a fully protected Rent Act tenancy. Getting vacant possession at the end of the fixed term was also dependent on the landlord having served the correct statutory notice within the last three months of the fixed term. Any failure to serve such notice meant that the tenancy would carry on to its next anniversary, when the landlord would have another chance to serve the required statutory notice to bring it to an end.

The absence of a booming private rented sector coupled with an adequate stock of public sector housing meant that the housing benefit budget was manageable. The only private tenants were those existing tenants whose long-term right to occupy and rent level were already protected under the 1977 Rent Act. Anyone else would be renting from a local authority or housing association, whose rent would already be fixed at an affordable level. As the 2015 Civitas Report states on page 12:

The widening affordability gap is illustrated by the growing number of people who are coming to rely on housing benefit. In 1988/89, at about the time that rent controls were abolished and council housing building went into terminal decline, the housing benefit bill was, in today's prices, £7.4 billion. Since then, however, the cost has more than trebled in real terms and now comes to about £24 billion. The number of claimants has risen too, by about a quarter (from just under four million to just over five million in 2013/14).

4 *Introduction*

The sea change came with the Housing Act 1988 which, for the first time in a quarter of a century, allowed private sector landlords to let on new assured shorthold tenancies, on which their rents would not be controlled and where landlords could recover vacant possession when they wanted. But this would not be a problem because a revitalised rented market meant that there would always be an ample supply of alternative accommodation for those displaced tenants to move into. Housing associations could also let on the new shorthold terms, although many have chosen to confer longer security of tenure through the contractual terms of their tenancies. Like the earlier protected shortholds, there were strict statutory procedures required to set up an 'assured shorthold', failing which the tenancy would default to a lifetime 'assured tenancy'. Provided these procedures were followed, the landlord could let on a fixed term of as little as six months and have the right to recover at any time thereafter on giving to the tenant not less than two months statutory notice. The Housing Act 1996 removed the specific legal formalities required to set up an assured shorthold tenancy and instead made assured shortholds the default tenancies for most short-term residential lettings.

Although originally introduced as part of Conservative Party policy to revitalise a private-rented housing market, assured shorthold tenancies survived the 1997–2010 Labour Governments without significant change and remain today the predominant mechanism for short- to medium-term lettings of residential accommodation. But local authorities have always operated within a different market.

Until the Housing Act 1980, local authority housing tenants had no statutory security of tenure. Council lettings were outside the scope of the 1977 Rent Act. It meant that the only protections which council tenants had were through common law principles of public law which had developed since the 1947 landmark Court of Appeal judgment in *Associated Picture Houses v Wednesbury Corporation* [1948] 1 KB 223.

The essence of *Wednesbury* was that any decision by a public authority could be struck down by the courts if in reaching its decision the public body:

- failed to have due regard to relevant considerations;
- had taken into account irrelevant considerations; or
- acted in a way which was so unreasonable that a reasonable public body – which had been properly advised – could not have acted in the same way.

It was the Housing Act 1980 which for the first time conferred statutory lifetime security of tenure on local authority tenants. But that security of tenure was still looser than that imposed by the 1977 Rent Act on private sector lettings, as there were no statutory rent controls. Provided tenants kept to the terms of their tenancies, they could now occupy their accommodation for life and pass on their tenancies to members of their families resident with them at their deaths. But it was the Housing Act 1980 which also introduced one other landmark reform: statutory right to buy.

Even under the Labour Government, which was in office before the May 1979 General Election took Margaret Thatcher to power, some councils were selling housing stock to their tenants at discounted prices. The Housing Act 1957 coupled with subsequent ministerial consents allowed them to do this. But it was something over which each council had control. There was no obligation to sell and it was for each local authority to determine the terms of sale. It meant there were some councils which offered generous sale terms to their tenants – whilst other councils refused to sell at all. To off-set existing council housing stock which was being sold, there was still at this time new stock being built. What the Housing Act 1980 did was to place all local authorities under the same obligation to sell existing housing stock to tenants who qualified and also to regulate the terms of each sale. It was part of the Government's commitment to wider home ownership. Unfortunately, the introduction of right-to-buy coincided with another 1980 Government policy: Michael Heseltine's moratorium on the building of new local authority housing stock.

The 'right' was available to 'secure' tenants who had occupied for a minimum qualifying period and discounts could be up to 60% depending on how long the tenant had previously been in occupation under their tenancy. The terms of sale meant that right-to-buy purchasers would have to repay the whole or part of their statutory discount if they resold within the first few years of their purchase. After the expiry of that short repayment period there was no restriction on when and to whom that property could be re-sold. The other feature of right-to-buy was that since 1st April 1990 financial regulations have prevented councils from reinvesting sale receipts in constructing new social housing. Section 59 of the Local Government and Housing Act 1989 required three quarters of that income to be set aside to pay off existing debt. That legislation is now contained within regulation 23 of the Local Authorities (Capital Finance and Accounting) (England) Regulations 2003 and later amendments.

Like assured shorthold tenancies, statutory right-to-buy survived the incoming Blair/Brown Governments of 1997–2010 although the level of discount was scaled back whilst the terms of sale were made marginally more onerous. As a result, the actual number of right-to-buy sales during that period dropped to a trickle.

But right-to-buy enjoyed a resurgence with the incoming Coalition Government of 2010, when qualifying and repayment periods were reduced and discounts increased. The Government also announced a commitment to extend generous right-to-buy discounts to housing association tenants, who hitherto had only enjoyed a more modest 'right to acquire', which had been introduced by the Housing Act 1996 and for which there was little take up. The only difference between that and Thatcher's right-to-buy was Cameron's assurance that homes sold under the new right-to-buy would be replaced by new social housing on a one-for-one basis. The problem with generous right-to-buy policies is that they act as a disincentive to local authorities trying to address housing need by developing new council housing stock for rent. What would be the point?

Save for a few statutory exceptions, any new housing stock which a council builds to meet long-term housing need and then lets out directly to its own tenants is immediately converted by the Housing Act 1985 into a secure tenancy carrying with it a statutory right-to-buy. After a three-year qualifying period, tenants can begin exercising their right-to-buy at increasing levels of discount as time elapses. And there is no guarantee that those homes sold under right-to-buy will remain forever in owner occupation. Once a home has been sold to a sitting tenant, there is in most cases nothing to stop that home being re-sold immediately by that former tenant to a private buy-to-let landlord. Yes – there may be some discount to repay. But there is little legally to prevent that sale taking place.

Current right-to-buy terms require an ex-tenant to offer to sell their home back to the council, at full market value, before selling on to a third party during the first ten years of purchase. But how many councils take up that offer after they had already paid away the bulk of their original capital receipt under set-aside? The end result is that as, over time, the new social housing is sold off, councils are eventually put in the position of having to rent back properties on their own estates in order to meet their statutory obligations. Paragraph 2.13 of the Greater London Assembly October 2013 Housing Committee Paper, 'Right to Build. What's Stopping Councils From Building More Housing' highlights the problem:

> *Perhaps the most egregious consequence of Right-to-Buy and abuse of the system has been the recycling of former council homes into the private rental sector. Hard evidence is difficult to come by but Mayor Sir Steve Bullock, for London Councils, suggested that conclusions drawn from research undertaken in Scotland, demonstrating that this had happened to a large proportion of ex-council stock, were also likely to apply in London. This can result in the absurd situation of councils having to rent back their old stock from new private landlords at much higher rents in order to fulfil their statutory duties. The increased costs are usually met by the benefits system.*

It is disappointing that the Housing White Paper has not taken the opportunity to address this disincentive and give councils and other registered providers the confidence they need to build out new social housing safe in the knowledge that those homes will be kept permanently available to meet housing need and bring down the cost of renting. Instead the White Paper does the opposite. Instead of exempting social housing new-build from right-to-buy, the White Paper promises to extend it to all social tenants, irrespective of whether they rent from a local authority or a registered provider.

Since publication of the Housing White Paper and as a result of the intervening 8th June 2017 General Election, the current Conservative Administration has lost its overall Parliamentary majority but remains in power as a minority government. Accordingly, the Queen's Speech presented to Parliament on 21st June 2017 was much stripped down from what it might otherwise have been if Theresa May had won her expected landslide. On housing, all the that the Queen had to say was: '*Proposals will be brought forward to ban unfair tenant fees, promote fairness and transparency in the housing market and help ensure more homes are built.*' There was no mention in that speech of right-to-buy or its extension to other social housing tenures. The May Government's commitment to extending right-to-buy in England is also out of step with what is currently happening in Scotland and Wales.

Right-to-buy ended for all council and housing association tenants in Scotland on 31st July 2016. As this chapter is being written, the Abolition of the Right to Buy and Associated Rights Bill is passing though Welsh National Assembly which, after a 12-month breathing space, will abolish right-to-buy across Wales. Existing discounts are in the meantime stripped back to £8,000 and one of the aims of the Welsh legislation is to:

> *Encourage social landlords to build or acquire new homes for rent, as the right-to-buy, preserved right-to-buy and right-to-acquire will not be exercisable by tenants who move into new social housing more than two months after the Bill receives Royal Assent, subject to certain exceptions.*

In the meantime, the continued existence of right-to-buy means that English councils cannot build and rent out new social housing directly. They need to work with a private sector partner or with some other intermediary organisation, such as a housing association or a special purpose company. It is then that intermediary organisation which will manage the newly built housing stock and let it out to persons nominated as being in housing need. Because that intermediary is not a local authority it will be outside the Housing Act

1985 and able to let on assured shorthold tenancies in the same way as any other private landlord.

Just one warning. Although many councils are regenerating in this way, the whole process is still legally untested. Can a local authority really exempt itself from tenant security and right-to-buy simply by setting up its own company to manage its housing stock? And what if this (or a future) Government can still muster enough Parliamentary votes to extend right-to-buy to a council's housing association partner? The 2015 Civitas Report advocates a return to statutory rent controls as a means of making housing affordable. We beg to disagree.

The current housing crisis is entirely the result of a distorted housing market in which the housing benefit system competes with private renters and in which first-time buyers are priced out by the buy-to-renters. It follows that the only sustainable solution is one which enables councils and other voluntary providers to meet affordable housing needs from within their own stock and without recourse to the private rented market. That market will remain to meet the demands of private renters. But it will no longer be the state-subsidised cash-cow which it is today.

This book looks at how a typical housing regeneration project might be structured to ensure that the accommodation provided is kept permanently available to meet long-term housing need. It is written for councillors, chief officers, prospective development partners and any property professional or student who may be coming to a housing regeneration project for the first time. It is intended to provide a route map pointing the way to the more detailed research, analysis and advice which may be required to work up a regeneration project.

1 The route map

There may be several reasons why a local authority may wish to carry out a housing regeneration. In many cases it will be a second or third generation project. An example is Camden Council's current third generation redevelopment of its Agar Grove Estate, to which Camden's Cabinet gave the go-ahead in December 2013 and which got planning permission five months later. The original Agar Grove Estate got its name from William Agar of Elm Lodge who, in the early 1800s, fought against the cutting of the Regent's Canal through his property. Following his death in 1838 his widow began granting building leases on the estate, which became known as Agar Town. But the residents of that settlement were later displaced with the building of the Midland Railway's St Pancras Station, with its associated tracks and goods yard. In the 1960s Camden Council carried out a redevelopment to provide 249 new homes and comprising a series of low/medium-rise blocks and an 18-storey tower block, which became known as Lulworth House. But by the date of the 2013 Cabinet decision it had become apparent that this 1960s development had also come to the end of its useful life. The problems were not social but physical. In paragraphs 3.3 and 3.4 of the statement of reasons to support a compulsory purchase order, the council explains:

> *3.3 The Estate is home to a stable and cohesive community including many householders who have lived there for a number of years and are established in the area. However, despite being a popular place to live, the existing stock suffers from a number of problems ranging from physical defects to the size, type and quality of the accommodation relative to modern housing needs. Furthermore, the existing configuration of the Estate represents an inefficient use of land given its accessible and sustainable location. All 249 homes on the Estate have very significant investment needs.*
>
> *3.4 The Estate currently comprises a series of free-standing blocks surrounded by areas of open space which were laid out in response to*

10 *The route map*

solar orientation but do not measure well against today's principles of good urban design and place-making. As a result the Estate comprises a series of 'objects in space' with a lack of definition between buildings and spaces; poor resolution of fronts and backs; poor legibility with expanses of green space with no clear programme of use; and an urban form which is detached from the wider area.

The current redevelopment comprises the demolition of all the low-rise buildings on the estate, apart from L & Q housing association blocks and the Agar Children's Centre. Enough new Camden Council homes will then be built for all existing tenants who wish to continue living at Agar Grove. Some of the new-build flats and refurbished flats in Lulworth will be sold outright or on shared ownership to cross-subsidise the rest of the redevelopment. The regeneration also includes communal gardens and play spaces.

A larger scheme is Hackney Council's rolling eight-year multi-site regeneration programme running from July 2011 to 2019 and which is forecast to deliver 2,485 new-build homes of which 1,236 will be affordable (comprising 717 homes for social rent and 519 homes for shared ownership). In addition, 195 social rented homes will be refurbished to a 30-year life standard and 80 leasehold homes will be externally refurbished. The scheme also has to cater for the additional demand for education, leisure, public realm, energy use, traffic and public transport, which will be assessed through the town planning process and addressed through planning obligations alongside on-site provision of facilities such as amenity space, play facilities and measures to reduce carbon footprint.

In September 2009 Hackney achieved Housing Investment Partner Status with the Homes and Communities Agency (HCA) entitling it to bid for an allocation of Social Housing Grant (SHG): for which it was allocated £10 million to build 115 homes for social rent under Round 1 of the bidding and a further £6.26 million to build 87 social rent homes under Round 2. Construction of those homes is now complete and occupied at Bridport (Colville Estate), Ottaway Court (now Dunnock Mews), Rendlesham House (now Goldcrest Mews); Alexandra National House; Brooklime House and Chervil House. Hackney then secured a further £4.26 million grant funding under the National Affordable Homes Programme 2011–2015, enabling the delivery of a further 93 social rent homes and 38 for shared ownership. However, the intention is that over the longer-term Hackney's regeneration programme will be completely self-funding and deliver a financial return to the council, which will be achieved through:

- residual land value created through the sale of units constructed for outright private sale;

- receipt of initial equity tranche sales and the subsequent rental stream from shared ownership homes;
- ring-fencing rental receipts at target rents from the new social affordable units; and
- mitigating right-to-buy repurchase costs through the provision of equity-swap arrangements.

But not all regeneration involves the replacement of post-war tower blocks. Perhaps a piece of council-owned land has become surplus to requirements, as council services and their operational requirements contract, and has become ripe for redevelopment. Perhaps there is a prospect of central government funding becoming available if development deadlines can be met. Often it is a combination of all of them.

Having identified a prospective housing regeneration project, the first formal step may be to present a report to the appropriate Cabinet or councillor committee seeking political support for the principle of regeneration and the allocation of a budget to pay professional fees to work up a detailed and costed scheme for final approval. That report may also outline possible options and seek authorisation for a tender exercise to find a potential development partner to carry out the construction and for a registered provider to manage the affordable housing once it has been constructed. That initial Cabinet or committee approval and budget will then enable the engagement of property professionals to work up a scheme and begin the process of tendering for a development partner.

Surveyors will be appointed to check that the land is physically capable of redevelopment and to provide valuations. Lawyers will check the titles to the land and its ownership and identify any third-party rights or interests which might inhibit the carrying out of development or which need to be re-acquired. In the case of the Agar Grove regeneration, this would include Camden Council's need to repurchase homes previously sold under right-to-buy as well as providing suitable alternative accommodation for existing council tenants who are still in occupation. Where such rights or interests are identified, it is those same lawyers who will need to advise on how those development constraints can be overcome.

The next stage is to put in hand a transparent procurement process to identify a potential development partner. That process will need to be compliant with European Rules and the council's own contract standing orders. Prospective development partners will be invited to bid against a development specification. Annexed to that specification may be drafts of any development agreement or other documentation which the successful appointee will be expected to sign.

However, before that appointment can actually take place, a second report will need to go back to Cabinet or the appropriate committee with a fully costed and worked-up scheme and a report on the bids received with a detailed recommendation as to which development partner should be appointed to implement the project.

Following that second resolution, the council will notify the prospective development partner that their bid has been accepted. From notification of that appointment, the council and the development partner will be in a formal contractual relationship, even if the development agreement itself has not yet been signed.

Before development can actually start, there are other preliminary hurdles which must first be overcome. Planning permission will first need to be applied for and obtained. If there are multiple third-party interests to be acquired, it may be appropriate to put a compulsory purchase order in place. There may also be roads and footpaths crossing the site which need to be stopped up to enable development to take place.

Only when all of these preliminary issues have been surmounted can the development-partner be allowed on site in accordance with the terms of the development agreement to commence and complete the redevelopment. On completion of the redevelopment, ownership of the appropriate parts of the site will be transferred by the local authority to the development partner or, as the case may be, the registered housing provider. The affordable housing will then be let by the housing association on assured shortholds or sold on shared ownerships to persons nominated by the local authority as being in housing need. The allocation criteria will be set out in a nomination agreement signed between the local authority and the registered provider.

Key to the success of any regeneration project is the support of the people whose lives it will directly affect. No programme of regeneration can succeed in the face of an entrenched and united campaign of opposition. It is why a programme of planned human engagement is just as important to a regeneration project as compliance with legal formalities. Someone whose home is being compulsory purchased will need to be convinced that there will be a better home waiting for them once construction is complete, that their community will not be broken up and that they will be no worse off financially. It means that councils embarking on a regeneration project must be able to offer a range of options to those people who will potentially be displaced, including the possibility of one-for-one swaps as an alternative to a cash payment.

It is a lucky project which goes entirely to plan. Most do not. It is why a project team must anticipate everything which could possibly go wrong, list them in a 'risk register' and put in place contingencies. That risk register will then need to be regularly updated as the project progresses. Some risks will fade as project milestones are reached, whilst other – previously unforeseen risks – may be added to the register. Typical risks for a regeneration project might include:

- insufficient interest amongst potential development partners;
- tenders for the construction work are higher than anticipated;
- planning permission is refused, delayed, or granted on terms so onerous that they undermine the financial viability of the project;
- difficulty in negotiating terms for the rationalisation of land interests required for site assembly;
- expected grant-funding required for the project is not forthcoming – or is less than expected or offered on more onerous terms;
- delay in finalising terms between the council and its development partner;
- unexpected physical constraints which add to the construction cost – such as the discovery of an underground cellar;
- uncertainties of continued member support for the project, particular in the face of an organised campaign of opposition by those residents most affected;
- a collapse in the housing market, which reduces the overall profitability of any project which is being cross-subsidised by the development of homes for private sale.

The 14th June 2017 Grenfell Tower tragedy also provides a stark reminder that risk does not end on practical completion – or when the last private-sale home is sold. It continues. At the time of writing, a public inquiry has been announced but has yet to take place into why more than 80 people lost their lives as a result of a flash-fire which consumed almost the whole of the 24-storey 67.30 metre high building and which was caused (it is believed) by flammable cladding installed during a 2012 £10 million refurbishment project designed to improve insulation and make the building warmer in winter and cooler in summer. Building services engineers, Max Fordham's, 17th August 2012 Sustainability and Energy Statement explained the purpose of the refurbishment: '*Poor insulation levels and air tightness on both the walls and windows at Grenfell Tower result in excessive heat loss during the winter months and addressing this issue is the primary driver behind the refurbishment.*' It added, '*The chosen strategy is to wrap the building in a thick layer of insulation and then overclad with a rain screen to protect the insulation from the weather and from physical damage.*'

The situation was not helped by a stay-put fire policy. A May 2016 *Grenfell Tower Regeneration Newsletter* advised residents:

> The smoke detection systems have been upgraded and extended. The Fire Brigade has asked us to reinforce the message that, if there is a fire

14 *The route map*

which is not inside your own home, you are generally safest to stay put in your home to begin with, the Fire Brigade will arrive very quickly if a fire is reported. The only reason you should leave your home is if the fire is inside your home.

It must be expected that the inquiry, when it happens, will consider not only the direct causes of the fire but also the extent to which that fire risk was – or should have been – foreseeable to those responsible for its installation. In that respect it is noteworthy that similar insulation materials were used in many other tower blocks across the UK and Europe. Each of those tower blocks will require extensive and urgent works to remove existing cladding and substitute a fire-resistant alternative. Because of the likely extent of those works there are also the associated logistical issues as regards the temporary rehousing of residents living in the blocks. An added complication is that many of the flats in those blocks will have already been sold under right-to-buy.

What is certain is that the conclusions of the public inquiry will have implications for all housing regeneration projects. A regeneration project team cannot be held responsible for everything which happens after a project has been delivered. Even if the project was problem-free at the point of delivery, subsequent lack of maintenance could risk health and safety. However, it is the job of a regeneration team to deliver a project which is free from inherent risk or defect, according to the state of scientific knowledge at the date the project is delivered.

There will be many variants on this model, but the fundamental routemap will always be the same. The good news is there is so much information about current regeneration projects which is freely available to download. Each one is a textbook providing ideas and knowhow for the next generation of projects. Examples of project documentation which is already in the public domain include: Cabinet reports and resolutions; compulsory purchase orders; statements of reasons; demolition notices; community engagement; planning reports and decisions: even complete development agreements.

2 Information gathering

If the starting point for any housing regeneration project is the idea, the next stage is to test the feasibility of that thought. This is initially a desktop information-gathering exercise. It is about trying to find out who owns what. Even if a local authority is redeveloping its own housing estate, it is unlikely that the council will own everything.

Some units may have previously been sold under right-to-buy. So, the council will need to buy them back. There may be electricity substations and other utility-owned services within the regeneration site. There may also be roads, public footpaths and public amenity areas. This particular desktop exercise would normally comprise:

- a review of Land Registry records;
- a review of such physical documentation as exists;
- standard conveyancing searches.

The assessment would need to be carried out by an experienced conveyancer with electronic access to Land Registry records. And all that conveyancer would need to begin that exercise is a red-line plan showing the location of the proposed regeneration site in relation to surrounding streets and landmarks. Using that red-line plan, the conveyancer will be able to search Land Registry records and provide a detailed report on the different ownerships which make up the regeneration site. As well as identifying ownerships, the 'title report' will also detail and highlight known documented third-party interests which might obstruct – or make more difficult or expensive – the process of carrying out a redevelopment. Those third-party interests might include contractual restrictions on the way land can be developed or used, the existence of private rights of way, or the rights of adjoining owners to use pipes, wires or other utility services running through the land.

The process of collecting title information is made easier by the process of land registration which exists in the UK and which means that most title information is available for instant download. Modern land registration began with the Land Registration Act 1862. But the scheme, as launched, was entirely voluntary and little used. Inner London became the first area of compulsory land registration in 1899. Compulsory registration means that every time unregistered land is sold, the purchaser is placed under an obligation to apply for first registration of their title. Until that registration takes place, title does not fully transfer to the new purchaser. Compulsory registration is therefore a piecemeal process. Unless and until a transaction takes place to trigger first registration, the land remains unregistered.

By contrast, title to unregistered land is evidenced by an examination of the physical title deeds in a system which has barely changed since medieval times. As the documentation is 'unregistered', the information contained within it is only accessible to the person or organisation holding the deeds.

Over the course of a century, compulsory land registration extended on a district-by-district basis until by December 1990 compulsory registration had extended across the whole of England and Wales. Before 1990 registered title information was private, which meant that it was only accessible by the registered land owner and anyone else whom they authorised to access the register. Such restricted access was deliberate to give registered land owners the same privacy as that enjoyed by unregistered landowners. But that changed when all registered titles were opened up to public access. It is that public access which now makes it possible to obtain documented title information quickly and with certainty. However, nearly 30 years after compulsory registration was rolled out across the remainder of the UK, approximately 18% of land still remains unregistered. There may be several reasons for this:

- The land belongs to institutional landowners such as local authorities, central government departments, religious institutions or charities. With no change in ownership – the requirement to register title would not have arisen.
- It comprises the subsoil of ancient highway, in which there has never been any documented ownership. Under conveyancing law, title to such subsoil is presumed to belong to the owners of properties fronting the highway, up to the median and subject to the right of the public to travel across the surface.

There are also some types of transaction which are exempt from the requirement to register because of their temporary nature. The clearest example of this are leases for terms not exceeding seven years, or with less than seven years unexpired on the date of any assignment. Such leases take effect as 'overriding interests', which mean that they bind the title even though they are not expressly mentioned. Other 'overriding interests' include the rights of persons in actual occupation of the property as well as public rights of way and any private rights of way or service easements which were never officially documented but acquired by long user. Rights of light belonging to neighbouring landowners provide another example of an overriding interest which can hamper the carrying out of any redevelopment which might materially reduce the flow of light to those windows. As the requirement to register leases of more than seven years did not enter conveyancing law until 13th October 2003, there are many older leases which remain unregistered even though they were granted for longer periods up to 21 years. For a lease granted out of an unregistered freehold, the requirement to register the leasehold interest only applied if it was granted for a period of more than 42 years.

What this means is that although registered title information provides a snapshot of land ownership on the date the information is provided, that information cannot be guaranteed as complete. It is why the due diligence review of physical title deeds is also recommended (to the extent that such documentation can be made available).

A starting point for anyone piecing together registered title information is to obtain a 'map search'. This is currently a free service provided by the Land Registry to anyone having access to the Land Registry Portal. From just a postcode, anyone using this service can obtain an online map of the immediate locality showing – tinted pink – all registered land in the vicinity. By ticking a box, title numbers can then be overlaid on that registered land. Starting from ground-zero, the map search provides a guide as to which particular titles should be investigated.

The next step is to apply for a Land Registry index map search: this involves uploading a plan of the land in question, together with a postcode and a brief description of its location. The Land Registry will then respond with a list of all title numbers which are applicable to the land in question, stating in each case whether those titles are freehold or leasehold. At one time the Land Registry would also have enclosed a map showing, by means of different colouring, which title numbers applied to which parts of the land, which greatly simplified the process of title investigation. But that information is no longer provided as standard. It can instead be purchased separately from Land Registry Commercial Services as an 'illustrative map'. The cost of an index map search can be as little as £4, more if there are a large number of titles. The cost of an illustrative map is always substantial and the buyer will be required to agree terms before the request will be actioned. Unlike the free map search, reliance can be placed on the results of the index map search in any conveyancing transaction.

Having obtained a list of relevant title numbers, the title information itself can be downloaded via the Land Registry Portal. At its most basic, this will

18 Information gathering

comprise firstly the register of title and secondly the title plan. The register of title is in fact three registers, namely: property register; proprietorship register; and charges register. The title plan will mark with a red line the boundaries of all the land comprised within that title and also show 'edged green' any areas of land formerly within that title which have since been sold off (indicating also the title numbers within which those lands are now comprised). The title plan will also cross-refer back to the register and indicate which parts of the land are affected by restrictive covenants, leases and, specifically, defined easements and wayleaves (such as drains or the routes of utility services) for which the register makes express reference. The information provided in a register of title can be summarised as follows:

- **Property register**: a brief description of the land remaining in the title (by cross-reference to the title plan), whether it is freehold or leasehold, as well as details of any documented rights which are enjoyed with the land (such as rights of way or service easements across adjoining land) and details of any corresponding third-party rights to which the land is subject.
- **Proprietorship register**: containing the name and address of the current registered proprietor as well as details of anything restricting that persons' right to deal with the property. When land is subject to mortgage, a mortgage lender will routinely insist on a 'restriction' preventing the owner from selling or leasing the land whilst it remains in mortgage.
- **Charges register**: which will list everything else in the nature of third-party rights which are recorded against the land. This list will commonly include any restrictive covenants, leases or financial charges affecting the registered title.

Any title register can only be as up to date as the last time any formal application was made to change the register, which will usually be the date of the last transaction involving the land. The Land Registry will not know that a registered proprietor has died, or changed address, or that a corporate owner has gone into liquidation unless anyone has troubled to notify it. For this reason, there are thousands of registered titles showing outdated information. A common example is that many local authority titles are still registered in the names of former urban and rural districts; Middlesex County Council; London County Council; the Greater London Council and many other corporate bodies which have long since disappeared as a result of successive local government reorganisations. Even the title plan can be decades out of date as it may still show the topography which existed on the date the land was first registered. So, a built-up area may still be shown on the title plan

Information gathering 19

as farm land. It is those topographical changes which can make it so difficult to accurately plot historic title information onto the plan of a modern housing estate. The problem will be worse if the land is still unregistered, when it may be a case of trying to transpose 19th century field boundaries onto a modern urban landscape.

As well as register entries and title plans, the Land Registry will also hold scanned copies of historic transfers and conveyances, current leases, mortgages and associated documentation referred to in the title entries, many of which are also available for instant download. Ideally the documentation which the Land Registry holds electronically should mirror the hard copy documents which would be found in a traditional deed packet. In practice the Land Registry will rarely hold copies of everything, but will still be able to provide the key information and documentation which is required for a due diligence title check.

Where land is unregistered, the first issue is to locate a deed packet containing the unregistered title documents. That may not be a problem where the local authority itself is the reputed owner. 'Investigating title' is then about reviewing title documentation going back at least 15 years or earlier to the last arms' length conveyance transferring title. That arms' length conveyance may itself cross-refer back to even earlier documents containing plans or restrictive covenants which may date back more than a century. When land is believed unregistered, it is even more important to carry out a Land Registry index map search to identify whether any of the land falls within an existing registered title or whether there is anything registered by a third party which may in any way inhibit a future first registration of the land in question. As well as the index map search, the other search (which specifically relates to unregistered land) is a K15 land charges search, which may reveal third-party interests recorded against the land which may not be readily apparent from the title deeds themselves.

As well as downloading and reviewing Land Registry information and checking the contents of deed packets, where available, no title investigation is complete without due diligence conveyancing searches. The purpose of these searches is to throw up information about anything of a public nature or relating to the availability of utility services or any known physical constraints which might impede a future redevelopment of the land. Like the downloading of Land Registry information, these searches can be made online through commercial search providers, such as Thames Water Property Service. These searches fall into the following three basic types:

- **Local land charges search and associated local authority enquires.** These are answered by the local authority's own local land charges team and are to obtain information of a public nature about the land

and any documented proposals which may affect it in the future. The statutory search will provide information registered as affecting the property, such as the existence of a smoke control order. It will also provide a history of planning applications granted or refused which affect the land, as well as the existence of any section 106 planning obligation. Perhaps more importantly, it may disclose specific financial charges registered against the land which have a statutory basis, such as the cost of default works where the owner has been in breach of a statutory notice. However, of more interest to conveyancers is the information provided in the additional enquiries (or CON 29). Information disclosed pursuant to those enquiries will include the status of adjoining roads and whether they are publicly adopted highways. It will also provide disclosure of any future road proposals and provide details of any statutory notices which have been served in relation to the property. It will also disclose the existence of any known public footpaths crossing the land (as shown in the definitive map). There is also the opportunity to raise optional additional enquiries including – crucially – whether any of the land is registered as common or village green.

- **Drainage and water search.** At one time, information about mains drainage and mains water supplies would have been included with the local authority enquiries. However, that changed in 1974 when drainage and water functions were taken out of local authority control by the Water Act 1973. The result is that those enquiries must now be made directly to the commercial organisations which are now responsible for those services following later privatisation. The basic information provided by a drainage and water search is whether a particular property is connected to a mains water supply and to mains drainage. However, more crucially for a regeneration project is the information it provides about any public sewers actually crossing the site and which may require diversion to enable the proposed redevelopment to proceed.
- **Environmental search.** A desktop search can provide no guarantee that land is not affected by chemical contamination. But it can provide a record of any historic uses which could have potentially created a risk of contamination (of which a former gas works provides the clearest example). Therefore, all such searches can do is indicate the level of risk of possible contamination. Such searches will also provide an indication of flood risk.
- **Utility searches.** The purpose of utility searches is to obtain, from relevant public utilities, maps of known pipes, wires, cables and other utility services crossing the land to be redeveloped. Much of that information may duplicate what is already shown on the title documentation as service easements or wayleaves. However, the purpose of utility searches

is to provide a snapshot of what physically exists on the ground, not how it is treated as a title issue.

As well as title constraints there may also be statutory restrictions on the way publicly owned property can be used or transferred. All publicly owned land would have at one time been acquired for a specific purpose. That purpose may still be evident from Land Registry entries or the original title deeds if the land has yet to be registered. The following is a common entry on many local authority titles, particularly of housing estates:

> RESTRICTION: *Except under an Order of the Registrar no disposition by the proprietor of the land is to be registered unless made in accordance with the Housing 1957 or some other Act or authority.*

The entry signifies that the land is held for a statutory purpose and that it cannot be sold, leased or mortgaged except in accordance with the statutory provisions under which it is held. Unless the Land Registry are satisfied that any transaction involving the land is specifically authorised by statute, that sale, lease or mortgage will not be registered and title will not legally transfer.

The Housing Act 1957 has been long since been replaced by the Housing Act 1985, although the title register itself may never have been updated. But it is not just the Housing Act 1957. Other land may have been acquired for the building of a school or for the purpose of recreation and the restriction will relate to the specific statutory provisions authorising that purchase. The use of the words, *'or other Act or authority'* is also recognition of the fact that under section 122 Local Government Act 1972 a local authority has power to 'appropriate' land within its ownership from one statutory purpose to another. However, any such 'appropriation' also requires adherence to applicable statutory formalities before it can become legally effective. Every statutory power has its limitations, not only as to the way publicly owned land can be used, but also as to the extent to which it can be sold or leased. It also follows that the terms of the restriction which is expressed on the registered title provides no guarantee that the land has not since been appropriated to another statutory purpose and is therefore subject to statutory restrictions which are different to those shown on title.

However, in the majority of cases, a registered title of publicly owned land may make no express reference to the statutory purposes for which it was originally acquired. For these reasons any due diligence title investigation must also apply professional judgment to identify the current statutory purpose for which the particular piece of land is held and the particular statutory constraints which will apply to any future transaction concerning

22 Information gathering

it. The most obvious clue is the way that the land has been developed and is actually being used. Land which has been built out and is currently occupied as a local authority housing estate will almost certainly be governed by the Housing Act 1985. Land built out as a school will be subject to the legislative regime applicable to schools and school playing-fields. But sometimes that statutory purpose is not obvious, particularly when a large title covers multiple public uses: such as a housing estate with a school; shops; amenity areas and car parks. It is then the job of the conveyancer to identify which statutory provisions apply to which parts of that massive title. Even where the statutory purpose of the original acquisition is not expressly stated, there may be other clues within the documentation as to the purpose for which it is held. This may include a record of right-to-buy leases granted out the title. Other clues may be found within individual deed packets or even historic committee reports or resolutions making express reference to the land and how it was acquired or appropriated.

3 Statutory constraints

This chapter contains a review of those statutory provisions which are specifically relevant to land held by local authorities. The term 'HRA' is the commonly used abbreviation for 'Housing Revenue Account' as defined by section 74 Local Government and Housing Act 1989. It is also the shorthand for any land currently held by local authorities under the Housing Act 1985. The HRA is a ring-fenced financial account which any local authority renting out housing directly is required to maintain and which is subject to tight statutory controls on what revenue goes into the account and what money is paid out of it. Section 74 also makes express reference to the Housing Act 1985 when describing the land to which it applies. The starting point for anyone dealing with HRA land is section 32 Housing Act 1985 (as amended by later legislation), the material parts of which state:

32 Power to dispose of land held for the purposes of this Part

(1) Without prejudice to the provisions of Part V (the right to buy) a local authority has power by this section, and not otherwise, to dispose of land held by them for the purposes of this Part.

(2) A disposal under this section may be effected in any manner but, subject to subsection (3), <u>shall not be made without the consent of the Secretary of State</u>.

(3) No consent is required for the letting of land under a secure tenancy or under an introductory tenancy or under what would be a secure tenancy but for any of the paragraphs 2 to 12 of Schedule 1 (tenancies other than long leases and introductory tenancies which are not secure).

(4) For the purposes of this section the grant of an option to purchase the freehold of, or any other interest in, land is a disposal and consent given to such a disposal extends to a disposal made in pursuance of the option.

24 *Statutory constraints*

The teeth is in the underlined words of section 32(2), which requires Secretary of State consent for any dealing with HRA land other than the grant of secure tenancies, introductory tenancies, or other residential tenancies exempted from security under Schedule 1 (for example service occupancies) and right-to-buy sales. The Minister in question is the Secretary of State for Communities and Local Government. Without more, a written application for consent would have to be made to the Secretary of State for almost any transaction involving HRA land other than residential tenancies and right-to-buy sales. However, section 32 has to be read together with section 34 (1)–(4) of the same Act, which states:

34 *Consents under ss 32 and 33*

(1) This section apples in relation to the giving of the appropriate national body's consent under section 32 or 33.

(2) Consent may be given –

 (a) either generally to all local authorities or to a particular authority or description of authority;
 (b) either in relation to particular land or in relation to land of a particular description.

(3) Consent may be given subject to conditions.

(4) Consent may, in particular, be given subject to conditions as to price, premium or rent to be obtained on the disposal including conditions as to the amount by which on a disposal of a house by way of sale or by the grant or assignment of a lease at a premium, the price or premium is to be discounted by the local authority.

Note the reference in section 34(2)(a) to consent being given generally to all local authorities. What this means is that instead of having to apply for a specific Secretary of State consent to implement a particular transaction, the local authority may be able to obtain the required authorisation from an existing general consent which applies to all local authority transactions of a particular type. At the time of writing the current general consents for all HRA land are comprised within a document issued by the DCLG in March 2013 and titled *The General Housing Consents 2013*. The document in fact comprises four separate general consents, namely:

A The General Consent for the Disposal of Land held for the purposes of Part II of the Housing Act 1985–2013;
B The General Consent for the Disposal of Dwelling-houses to Tenants who have acquired the Right to Buy acquiring with others 2013;

C The General Consent for the Disposal of Non-Part II Dwelling-houses 2013;
D The General Consent for the Disposal of Reversionary Interests in Houses and Flats 2013.

Each of these four consent classes is then sub-divided into sub-categories, each with its own terms and conditions. The issue is then to find the particular category which best fits the transaction in hand. If the proposed transaction falls outside any of the listed consent categories, a specific application for Secretary of State consent may still be required. For the purposes of this chapter (and for estate regeneration generally) we are only concerned with sub-categories A3.1.1 and A3.2 of the Class A General Consent, which state:

A3.1.1 A local authority may, subject to paragraph 3.1.2, dispose of land for a consideration equal to its market value. Para 3.1.2 disapplies the consent to a proposed disposal of land occupied under a secure, introductory or demoted tenancy to a non-local authority landlord. The other A3.1.1 qualifier is that the land cannot be sold at an undervalue. It means that if the local authority wishes to pass across HRA land to another party at a nil or reduced consideration, it must find another General Consent within which to slot the transaction.

A3.2 A local authority may dispose of vacant land. For the purpose of A.3.2 land is 'vacant' if either there are no dwellings built on it or any dwellings which have previously built have either been demolished or are no longer capable of human habitation and are due to be demolished. The key difference between A.3.2 and A.3.1 is that the sale does not have to be a market value. Therefore a local authority could use A.3.2 to transfer vacant HRA land to a housing association at nil value.

Further assistance can be found in the very wide section 24 Local Government Act 1988 as qualified by section 25, which states:

24 Power to provide financial assistance for privately let housing accommodation

(1) Subject to Section 25 below, a local housing authority shall have power to provide any person with financial assistance for the purposes of, or in connection with, the acquisition, construction, conversion, rehabilitation, improvement, maintenance or management (whether by that person or by another) of any property which is or is intended to be privately let as housing accommodation.

26 *Statutory constraints*

(2) For the purposes of this section and section 25 below a local authority may provide a person with financial assistance if they do or agree to do any of the following, that is to say –

(a) Make a grant or loan to that person;

(b) Guarantee or join in guaranteeing the performance of any obligation owed to or by that person;

(c) Indemnify or join in indemnifying that person in respect of any liabilities, loss or damage; or

(d) If that person is a body corporate, acquire share or loan capital in that person

25 Consent required for provision of financial assistance etc

(1) Subject to the following provisions of this section, a local authority shall neither –

(a) exercise the power conferred by section 24 above; nor

(b) so exercise any other power (whether conferred before or after the passing of this Act) as to provide any person, for the purposes of or in connection with the matters mentioned in subsection (1) of that section, with any financial assistance or with any gratuitous benefit, except under and in accordance with a consent given by the Secretary of State.

The two general consents issued under section 25 of the 1988 Act are *the general consents under section 25 of the Local Government Act 1988 (local authority assistance for privately let housing) 2010 and 2014.* The two are virtually identical save that the 2010 consent relates to financial assistance to registered housing providers, whilst the 2014 consent extends such financial assistance to other organisations. The 2010 consents (so far as applicable to housing regeneration) can be summarised as follows:

A **The general consent under section 25 of the Local Government Act 1988 for the disposal of land to registered providers of social housing 2010 (as amended)**

A1 A local authority may provide a registered provider, for the purposes of or in connection with the matters mentioned in section 24(1) of the 1988 Act, with any financial assistance or any gratuitous benefit consisting of:

(a) The disposal to that registered provider of land for:

(i) Development as housing accommodation or as housing accommodation and other facilities which are intended to

Statutory constraints 27

> benefit mainly the occupiers of the housing accommodation; or
>> (ii) The provision of access to land used or to be developed as housing accommodation; or
>
> (b) The grant to that registered provider of any easement or right appurtenant to land used or to be developed as housing accommodation

A2 Consent is given on condition that

> (a) any housing accommodation on the land when the disposal is made is vacant and that the terms of the disposal provide that the housing accommodation (other than any accommodation which has been developed pursuant to the terms of the disposal) shall not be used again as housing accommodation and shall be demolished;
> (b) Completion of the disposal is by transfer of the freehold, assignment of a lease with an unexpired term of 99 years or more or grant of a lease for a term of 99 years or more; and
> (c) The terms of the disposal provide that the development of any housing accommodation on the land shall be completed by a date which is not more than three years after completion of the disposal, but provision may be made for that date to be extended in the event of circumstances beyond the registered provider's control;
> (d) The terms of the disposal provide that any housing accommodation to be developed on the land shall be:
>
>> (i) let by the registered provider as social housing [meaning low cost rental accommodation as defined by **section 69 Housing and Regeneration Act 2008**] or a shared ownership lease or lease for the elderly or used as temporary accommodation for homeless persons; or
>> (ii) used as a hostel; or
>> (iii) occupied by persons who, on account of mental illness or handicap, are receiving support from a local social services authority; and
>> (iv) the local authority are not, under any agreement or other arrangement made on or before the disposal, entitled to manage or maintain any of the housing accommodation to be developed on the land.

A3 states that the occupancy condition specified in A2(d) above need not be binding on any mortgagee of the land or any person whose title is derived through such a mortgagee.

28 Statutory constraints

'Mortgagee exemption clauses' (as these are known) mean that it can never be guaranteed that the dwellings will remain forever as affordable housing. If the registered housing provider defaults on its mortgage obligations, the mortgage lender is then free to repossess the land (and any dwellings built on it) and sell on the open market to realise its security. However, the commercial reality is that without mortgagee exemption clauses, many schemes simply could not be funded. Many mainstream mortgage lenders will refuse to accept occupancy restrictions which could restrict their ability to obtain the best price when realising their securities. For more guidance on what mainstream mortgage lenders will – or will not – accept, refer to what is now the *UK Finance Mortgage Lenders' Handbook*, which is available as a continually updated online resource. However, a mortgagee's powers to force a sale of a registered provider's social housing stock is tempered by the moratorium provisions contained in the Housing and Regeneration Act 1988 (as amended) and Part 4 Chapter 5 of the Housing and Planning Act 2016.

> *A4 provides a £10 million annual cap on the total amount of financial assistance which a local authority can provide under the A1 Consent, as certified by the chief executive, chief legal officer or a qualified valuer employed or engaged by the authority. The value of financial assistance or gratuitous benefit provided is then calculated as being the difference between the open market unrestricted value of the land if sold on the open market and what (if anything) is actually received by the local authority for the disposal.*
>
> *A5 makes clear that a project which is authorised by A1 of this General Consent does not require any further consent to disposal by virtue of section 26(4) Town and Country Planning Act 1959 [but not section 233 Town and Country Planning Act 1990], section 123(2) Local Government Act 1972 (see below) or section 32(2) or 43(1) Housing Act 1985.*

The net effect is that if the transaction falls within A1 of this general consent, the local authority is not concerned with the limitations of the general housing consents 2013. Note also that the 2010 general consents also include the following additional consents under section 25, which are summarised as they are not considered directly relevant to a comprehensive scheme of housing regeneration:

> *B General consent for the disposal of dwelling-houses to registered providers for refurbishment;*
>
> *C General consent for financial assistance (not involving the disposal of an interest and property) to any person: for any of the matters mentioned in*

section 24(1) of the 1988 Act; of in exercise of any power conferred by section 48 Local Government Act 1985 [grants to voluntary organisations] or towards works to a project, for which the Secretary of State has already approved grant funding under section 1 Local Government Grants (Social Need) Act 1969.
D   General consent for small amounts of assistance or gratuitous need comprising the disposal of a dwelling-house or hostel to be occupied by persons who have a special need.
E   General consent for the disposal of residential care homes.

AA. The general consent under section 25 of the Local Government Act 1988 for the disposal of housing revenue account land 2014

This mirrors general consent A of the 2010 consents, save only that:

- it enables the disposal of land to anyone, not just registered providers;
- it relates only to the transfer of HRA land and, in that respect, is narrower than the 2010 consent, which applies to any land;
- it requires an obligation on the transferee to ensure that any housing development on the land is privately let as housing accommodation as defined by section 24(3) Local Government Act 1988.

The only other general consent within the same document is the general consent under section 25 of the Local Government Act 1988 for the disposal of dwelling-houses to registered providers of social housing 2014 (which relates to the disposal of vacant dwellings to registered providers for renovation and letting). Before leaving the Housing Act 1985, there is one final section of that Act which is relevant to housing regeneration.

Many housing regeneration projects involve an initial appropriation of land from HRA to planning purposes before onward transfer of the vacant site to the development partner to commence demolition and reconstruction. The reasons why such appropriation will assist future redevelopment is explained in Chapter 6 of this book. But for now, we look at section 19 of the 1985 Act which states:

19   Appropriation of land

(1) A local Housing Authority may appropriate for the purposes of this Part any land for the time being vested in them or at their disposal and the authority have the same powers in relation to land so appropriated as they have in relation to land acquired by them for the purposes of this Part.

(2) where a local Housing Authority have acquired or appropriated land for the purposes of this Part they shall not without the consent

Statutory constraints

> of the Secretary of State, appropriate any part of the land consisting of a house or part of a house for any other purpose.
> (3) the Secretary of State's consent may be given.
>
> (a) either generally to all local Housing authorities or to a particular authority or description of all authority, and
> (b) either in relation to particular land or in relation to land of a particular description.
> and it may be given subject to conditions.

All of the general consents referred to above relate to the *sale* of HRA land. None of those general consents make any passing reference to 'appropriation'. At the current time there are no general consents relating specifically to appropriation. It means that any local authority intending to appropriate land from HRA to planning (or indeed to any other statutory purpose)) has to look back to section 19 and form a view as to whether an express application needs to be made for a Secretary of State consent to cover the particular appropriation. However, it will also be apparent from a close reading of section 19 that a requirement for Secretary of State consent will *only* be necessary where the land to be appropriated includes a dwelling-house or part of a dwelling-house. The immediate direct effect of an appropriation from housing to planning is to bring the land within the constraints of the Town and Country Planning Act 1990 (as amended) of which the following provisions are relevant:

> **226 Compulsory acquisition of land for development and other planning purposes [Summarised]**
>
> (1) a local authority to which this section applies [being a county, a district or a unitary] shall, on being authorised to do so by the Secretary of State have power to acquire compulsorily any land in their area:
>
> > (a) if the authority think that the acquisition will facilitate the carrying out of development, re-development or improvement on or in relation to the land, or
> > (b) which is required for a purpose which it is necessary to achieve in the interests of the proper planning of an area in which the land is situated
> >
> > > (1A) But a local authority must not exercise the power under paragraph (a) of subsection (1) unless they think that the development, re-development or improvement is likely to contribute to the achievement of the promotion or improvement of the economic, social or environmental well-being of their area

Statutory constraints 31

(2) – relates to Crown land

(3) Where a local authority exercise their power under Subsection (1) in relation to any land, they shall, on being authorised to do so by the Secretary of State, have power to acquire compulsorily –

(a) any adjoining land which is required to execute works for facilitating its development or use; or

(b) where that land forms part of a common or open space or fuel or field allotment, any land which is required for the purpose of being given in exchange for the land which is being acquired

(4) it is immaterial by whom the local authority propose that any activity or purpose mentioned in Subsection 1 or 3(a) should be undertaken or achieved

Subsections (5) to (9) contain supplementary provisions

227 Acquisition of Land by agreement

Empowers a local authority to acquire by agreement any land which it could acquire compulsorily under section 226.

Section 228 deals with compulsory acquisition by the DCLG

232 Appropriation of land held for planning purposes

(1) Where land has been acquired or appropriated by a local authority for planning purposes and is for the time being held by them for the purposes for which it was so acquired or appropriated, the authority may appropriate the land for any purpose for which they are or may be authorised in any capacity to acquire land by virtue of or under any enactment not contained in this part or in Chapter V of Part 1 of the Planning (Listed Buildings and Conservation Areas) Act 1990;

(2) Land which consists of or forms part of a common and is held or managed by a local authority in accordance with a Local Act may not be appropriated under this section without the consent of the Secretary of State.

(3) Such consent (under 2 above) may be given in respect of a particular appropriation or to a class of appropriations and may be subject to or free from conditions or limitations.

(4) Before appropriating, under this section, any land which consists of or forms part of an open space, a local authority must first publish their intention to do so in a local newspaper for at least two

32 Statutory constraints

consecutive weeks and consider any objections received. Mirroring Section 123(2) Local Government Act 1972 (see below). (5) and (6) contain supplemental provisions.

233 Disposal by local authorities of land held for planning purposes

(1) Where any land has been acquired or appropriated by a local authority for planning purposes and is for the time being held by them for the purposes for which it was so acquired or appropriated, the authority may dispose of the land to such person, in such manner and subject to such conditions as appear to them to be expedient in order-

   (a) to secure the best use of that or other land and any buildings or works which have been, or are to be, erected, constructed or carried out on it (whether by themselves or by any other person), or
   (b) to secure the erection, construction or carrying out on it of any buildings or works appearing to them to be needed for the proper planning of the area of the authority.

(2) Land which consists of or forms part of a common, or formerly consisted of or formed part of a common, and is held or managed by a local authority in accordance with a Local Act shall not be disposed of under this section without the consent of the Secretary of State.

(3) The consent of the Secretary of State is also required where the disposal is to be for a consideration less than the best that can be reasonably be obtained and is not –

   (a) the grant of a term of seven years or less or.
   (b) the assignment of a term of years of which seven years or less are unexpired at the date of the assignment.

(4) Before disposing under this section any land which consists of or forms part of an open space, a local authority –

   (a) shall publish a notice of their intention to do so for at least two consecutive weeks in a newspaper circulating in the area; and
   (b) shall consider any objections to the proposed disposal which may be made to them.

(5) In relation to land acquired or appropriated for planning purposes for a reason mentioned in section 226(1) or (3), the powers conferred by this section on a local authority, and on the Secretary of State in respect of the giving of consent to disposals under

this section, shall be so exercised as to secure to relevant occupiers, so far as may be practicable, a suitable opportunity for accommodation.

(6) A person is a relevant occupier if –

  (a) he was living or carrying on business or other activities on any such land is mentioned in that subsection which the authority have acquired as mentioned in subsection (1)
  (b) he desires to obtain accommodation on such land, and
  (c) he is willing to comply with any such requirements of the authority as to the development and use of such land

(7) In subsection (5) a suitable opportunity for accommodation means, in relation to any person, an opportunity to obtain accommodation on the land in question which is suitable to his reasonable requirements on terms settled with due regard to the price at which such land has been acquired from him.

(8) In relation to any such land as is mentioned in Subsection (1) this section shall have effect to the exclusion of Section 123 Local Government Act 1972 (disposal of land by principal councils).

234 Disposal by Secretary of State of land acquired under s.228

(1) The Secretary of State may dispose of land held by him and acquired by him or any other Minister under section 228 to such person, in such manner and subject to such conditions as appear to him to be expedient.

(2) In particular, the Secretary of State may under subsection (1) dispose of land held by him for any purpose in order to secure its use for that purpose.

235 Development of land held for planning purposes

[Paraphrased] *gives local authorities general power to carry out construction works on land acquired or appropriated for planning purposes.*

The Local Government Act 1972 (as amended) is the default legislation governing land which is either not specifically held under other legislation or where that other legislation does not include specific powers to acquire land either by agreement or compulsory purchase. The 1972 Act regime is generally less restrictive than for land held under specific legislation such as the Housing or Planning Acts. But there are still some anomalies when in specific instances it is more restrictive than other legislation. An example is

34 Statutory constraints

A.3.2 of the general housing consents 2013 which places no requirement on local authorities to obtain the best price when selling vacant land. Contrast that with section 123 Local Government Act 1972 which imposes a general requirement on local authorities to obtain the best price when selling any interest in land which is more than the grant of a lease for more than seven years. Set out below are the relevant provisions of the 1972 Act relating to the holding and disposal of land by local authorities.

120 Acquisition of land by principal councils [Paraphrased]

(1)   For the purposes of any statutory function or for the benefit improvement or development of its area a principal council may acquire by agreement any land whether situated inside or outside its area.

(2)   Allows a principal council to acquire land notwithstanding that it is not immediately required for the statutory purpose for which it was acquired.

(3)–(5) contain supplementary provisions

121 Acquisition of land compulsorily by principal councils [Paraphrased]

Allows a council to acquire by compulsory purchase any land for which it is authorised to acquire by agreement for any statutory function. But note that the power of compulsory purchase does not apply to land only required for the benefit improvement or development of its area. Any compulsory purchase of land is also subject to confirmation by the secretary of state [see below].

122 Appropriation of land by principal councils [Paraphrased]

This is the main power allowing a local authority to appropriate land from one statutory purpose to another statutory purpose. The qualifier is that the land is no longer required for the statutory purpose for which it was originally acquired. Subsection 2 prevents a local authority from appropriating land forming part of a common or fuel or field garden allotment unless the area of that land does not exceed 250 square yards in aggregate and before making the appropriation the local authority first advertises its intention to do so for two consecutive weeks in a local newspaper and considers any objections received in response to that advertisement. A local authority is also prevented from appropriating land consisting of all forming part of open space unless they first advertise their intention to do so for two successive weeks identifying the land in question and considering any objections received. Compliance with those legal formalities also frees that open space from any public trust arising only from its previous open space designation.

123 Disposal of land by principal councils [Set out in full]

(1) Subject to the following provisions of this section a principal council may dispose of land held by them in any manner they wish.

(2) Except with the consent of the Secretary of State a council shall not dispose of land under this section, otherwise than by way of a short tenancy [being not more than seven years] for a consideration less than the best that can reasonably be obtained

(2A) A principal council may not dispose of land under subsection (1) consisting or forming part of an open space unless before disposing of the land they cause notice of their intention to do so specifying the land in question to be advertised for two consecutive weeks in a newspaper circulating in the area in which the land is situated and consider any objections to the proposed disposal which may be made to them.

(2B) [paraphrased] where by virtue of subsection (2A) above a council dispose of land which is held either for the purpose of section 164 Public Health Act 1875 (pleasure grounds) or section 10 Open Spaces Act 1906 (duty of local authority to maintain open spaces and burial grounds) the land shall by virtue of the disposal be freed from any trust arising solely by virtue of its being held in trust for enjoyment by the public in accordance with section 164 or as the case may be section 10.

It will be seen from the above that the key principles of the provisions listed above are that:

- In the main the 1972 legislation does not exist in isolation but supports other statutory functions. The only circumstances when the section 120 power to purchase is 'stand alone' is when the land is required by a local authority for the benefit, improvement or development of its area (and even then there is no corresponding power of compulsory purchase).
- The express powers listed above only benefit principal councils (being counties, county boroughs unitaries and districts).
- The fact that land is open to public access is not a bar to appropriation or disposal provided that the required statutory formalities have been complied with.
- The general rule is that the transfer of the freehold or lease for more than seven years must be at the best price recently obtainable (unless

the Secretary of State has previously authorised sale at a nil or reduced value).

The regime for the acquisition, appropriation and disposal of land by town and parish councils is set out in sections 124–127 of the Local Government Act 1972. In the main, these mirror the powers of acquisition, appropriation and disposal for principal councils, save that towns and parishes cannot compulsory purchase land directly. They must instead request the relevant principal council to exercise its compulsory purchase powers on behalf of (and at the expense of) the town or parish seeking the exercise of those powers.

So that local authorities do not have to apply specifically for Secretary of State consent every time they wish to transfer land at an undervalue, the then Office of the Deputy Prime Minister, issued *Circular 06/03: Local Government Act general disposal consent (England) 2003: disposal of land for less than the best consideration that can reasonably be obtained*. The Circular replaced an earlier Circular 6/93 supplemented by advice given by letter on 11th December 1988. The 2003 general consent remains in force at the time of writing. The text of the 2003 consent can be summarised as follows:

1 *The First Secretary of State ('the Secretary of State') in exercise of the powers conferred by sections 123(2), 127(2) and 128(1) of the Local Government Act 1972 hereby gives consent to a disposal of land otherwise than by way of a short tenancy by a local authority in England in the circumstances specified in paragraph 2 below.*
2 *The specified circumstances are:*

   (a) The local authority considers that the purpose for which the land is to be disposed is likely to contribute to the achievement of any one or more of the following objects in respect of the whole or any part of its area or of all or any persons resident or present in its area:

   (i) The promotion or improvement of economic well being
   (ii) The promotion or improvement of social well being
   (iii) The promotion or improvement of environmental well being; and

   (b) The difference between the unrestricted value of the land to be disposed of and the consideration for the disposal does not exceed £2,000,000 (two million pounds).

Any local authority intending to dispose of land at less than market value is advised by paragraph 17 of the Circular to obtain a realistic 'red book'

Statutory constraints 37

valuation of the land to be transferred in accordance with the methodology set down in the Technical Appendix to Circular 06/03 *Technical Appendix: Valuations for the Purpose of Determining Whether Proposed Land Disposals Under The Terms of the Local Government Act 1972 Fall Within the Provisions of the General Disposal Consent 2003*. In assessing unrestricted value, the valuer must ignore the reduction in value caused by any voluntary condition imposed by the authority.

The remainder of this chapter provides a summary of some other (usually more restrictive) powers for which local authorities may hold land. The list is not exhaustive but includes the following:

- *Education land.* Under Schedule 1 Academies Act 2010 (as amended) local authorities are required to obtain Secretary of State consent before any sale of a freehold or leasehold interest in land held by that local authority and which has been used for any school within the previous eight years. In addition, local authorities intending to dispose of playing fields need Secretary of State consent under section 77 School Standards and Framework Act 1998. Three general consents have been issued under that legislation namely: the School Playing Fields General Disposal and Change of Use Consent (No 5) 2014; the Academies General Disposal and Appropriation Consent (No 2) 2012; and the General Consent for the Disposal of Playing Fields by Restriction 2011. Even where school land has previously been transferred on a 125-year lease to an academy, the restrictions will still apply to the council's retained freehold interest. There will in addition be restrictions in the academy's own lease governing disposal or change of use as well as the academy's need to obtain Secretary of State consent under its 'funding agreement' for any future transfer of its leasehold interest.
- *Allotment land.* Section 8 Allotments Act 1925 states that where a local authority has purchased or appropriated land for use as allotments, the local authority shall not sell, appropriate, use or dispose of the land for any purpose other than use for allotments without the consent of the Secretary of State. Such consent may be given unconditionally or subject to such conditions as the Secretary of State thinks fit but shall not be given unless the Secretary of State is satisfied that adequate provision will be made for allotment holders displaced by the actions of the local authority or that such provision is unnecessary or not reasonably practicable.
- *Public access land.* This term is used generically in this book to describe not only land formally allocated for recreation use under section 164 Public Health Act 1875 or the Open Spaces Act 1906 but also to any other publicly owned land which is open to unrestricted public access

(with the exception only of common land or town/village green: see below). We have already seen from section 123(2A) Local Government Act 1972 that public access land can be sold or appropriated for other purposes provided that the intended disposal or appropriation is first advertised and consideration given to any objections received. However, whilst compliance with appropriate statutory formalities will free the land from any public trust arising only from its open space designation, there may be other covenants or restrictions on the title documentation itself in favour of other third parties (for example the Playing Fields Association) whose concurrence may be required before the land can be sold or appropriated for other purposes.

- *Highway land.* If the council has local highway functions, it will control land in its capacity as highway authority. But that does not mean that the local authority will own the land which it controls. In most cases it will not. In fact, the routes of many ancient highway are not in any documented ownership. But the fact that land is an adopted highway (or even an unadopted public right of way) will mean that it cannot be developed or used for other purposes unless the appropriate statutory procedures are put in place to secure the extinguishment or diversion of those public highway rights.
- *Charity land.* Local authorities frequently own land not in their own right but as the trustee of a charitable trust. The real owners of that land are those members of the public for whom the trust was set up to serve. It follows that such land cannot be sold or used for other purposes except in accordance with the terms of the original deed setting up the trust or by using other statutory powers contained within the Charities Act 2011 or in accordance with a scheme approved by the Charity Commission. The fact that the council holds land only in its capacity as trustee may not always be immediately apparent from the title register, although often it is. Any proposed dealing with charity land requires meticulous review of the original document setting up the charitable trust. Even when land can be sold under the express terms of the trust or under the Charities Act 2011, the proceeds of sale must then be applied only for the purposes of the trust.
- *Common land and village green.* Common land is technically land which is subject to rights of common in favour of any person. In many cases, such land continues to be administered under the particular 18th or 19th century Inclosure Act under which it was created. Since 1965 such land has been subject to a national scheme of registration contained in the Commons Registration Act 1965 and latterly by the Commons Act 2006. Town and village green is subject to similar registration requirements and relates to land over which there is an established

public right of recreation, usually as a result of long user. Although town/village green has the appearance of being publicly owned land, in most cases ownership does not vest with a local authority but with the 'lord of the manor'. Surprisingly such lordships can still be bought and sold on the open market, with the privileges which come with such ownership. The current legislation governing commons and village greens is the Commons Act 2006, which also restricts the way such land can be enclosed or developed.

- *Statutory green belt.* This is not to be confused with what is generally described as green belt within modern planning legislation: meaning land on which national and local planning policies prohibit development to prevent urban sprawl. Statutory green belt predates the Town and Country Planning Act 1947, which established modern planning controls, and is controlled instead by the Green Belt (London and Home Counties) Act 1938. Such land was originally acquired by local authorities (or several local authorities acting jointly) with the specific aim of keeping it open and undeveloped. The local authorities responsible for the original purchase of the land (or their statutory successors) are known as 'contributing authorities'. In most cases it will be immediately apparent from the register of title or other title documentation if land is held under the 1938 Act. Sections 5 and 10 of the Act prevent statutory green belt from being sold or developed without consent from the Secretary of State. Such consent cannot be given unless all the contributing authorities are in agreement. Most originating documentation establishing statutory green belt will also contain detailed covenants on the way that land can be used.

4 Development options

There is nothing in law to prevent a local housing authority building out new social housing on its own land and managing it directly. Section 9 Housing Act 1985 states:

(1) A local housing authority may provide housing accommodations by-

   (a) erecting houses or converting buildings into houses on land acquired by them for the purposes of this Part, or
   (b) by acquiring houses.

(2) An authority may alter enlarge repair or improve a house so erected, converted or acquired

(3) These powers may be exercised in relation to land acquired for the purpose of

   (a) disposing of houses provided or to be provided on the land; or
   (b) disposing of the land to a person who is interested in providing housing accommodation on it.

(4) A local housing authority may not under this part provide a cottage with a garden of more than one acre.

(5) Nothing in this act shall be taken to require (or to have at any time required) a local housing authority itself to acquire or hold any house or other land for the purposes of this part.

Section 10 of the 1985 Act (paraphrased) *states that a local housing authority may fit out, furnish and supply a house provided by them under this Part with the required furniture, fittings and conveniences. It may also sell or supply under a hire purchase agreement [as defined in the Consumer Credit Act 1974] furniture for the occupants of houses so provided and for that purpose buy furniture.*

Section 11(paraphrased) *gives an authority power to provide meal and refreshment facilities (but not sale of alcohol) and for laundering* *and laundry services as accords to the needs of housing occupants and make reasonable charges.*

Section 11 *(paraphrased) enables the provision of welfare services according to the needs of occupants together with power to make reasonable charges.*

Section 12 of the 1995 Act *enables a local authority either alone or with another person and with the Secretary of State's consent to maintain in connection with the provision of housing accommodation-*

(a) buildings adapted for use as shops
(b) recreation grounds
(c) other buildings with a beneficial purpose for housing occupants.

Although theoretically possible, it is difficult to find any recent examples of a local housing authority actually using its section 9 powers to directly construct and then manage new social housing as part of its own housing stock. There would be disadvantages in doing so. Any new housing stock built under section 9 and then managed directly would become part of the local authority's housing revenue account, with the consequences which flow from that. The Housing Act 1985 would apply automatically to any lettings of that new-build. Tenancies granted would either be secure or non-secure according to the reason for each particular letting. Secure tenancies would carry with them the statutory discounted right to buy. The management of the housing stock would be subject to the statutory constraints of the housing revenue account. Those HRA constraints are less since the government abolished housing revenue account subsidy in England by section 167 Localism Act 2011 and replaced it with a requirement for HRAs to be self-financing. It means that within the terms of any government borrowing cap, a local housing authority could borrow against its HRA to fund the cost of build housing.

Even where a local authority builds out housing directly under its Housing Act powers, it will still need to procure a building contractor to carry out the construction work. However, it will be the local authority client which retains full control of the project as well as any risks associated with it. Under its Housing Act powers, a local authority can only build new housing for rent or shared ownership, not for outright sale.

A variant of the direct build model is where a local housing authority constructs and manages its new housing stock through an intermediary council-controlled company. Because the company is constitutionally separate from the controlling local authority, any housing which it builds or manages will be outside the HRA. Such housing will not be governed by the Housing Act 1985 but instead by the Housing Act 1988 (as amended) which governs the private lettings market. Residential lettings will be on the basis of market-rent assured shortholds, not secure tenancies. There will be no statutory right to buy (though possibly a statutory right to acquire under the Housing Act 1996). Without long-term security of tenure, shorthold lettings can be terminated on as little as two months' statutory notice. Any rental subsidy will be through the housing benefit system not through a discounted rent levels.

One local authority which has adopted this variant is Conservative-controlled Wealden District Council, which has opted to set up its own housing and regeneration company both to acquire existing houses as well as to build new housing for outright sale and for market rent. Its stated purpose is to fill a gap in the housing market which it is felt disadvantages younger people striving to get on the housing ladder as well as older people who wish to trade down to smaller accommodation. The council set out its vision in its 2015–2019 corporate plan, which is to provide more homes that local people can afford, maintaining a balance between rural settlements and market towns, one option being for the council to set up its own housing company to develop housing and thereby create regeneration and growth. Its Cabinet approved an officer report setting out the principle of the scheme on 7th September 2016. The aim of the company (described in the report as Wealden Housing and Regeneration Company (WHRC)) was to generate income for the council; to become a self-financing body, and to promote home ownership and regenerate areas within the Wealden district. Whilst the core aim is to develop housing for outright sale, rent-to-buy and shared ownership, the report also recognised that the option of market rent would also need to be included to meet the needs of people unable to bridge the gap between their income and the cost of housing, if only on a temporary basis. It was also envisaged that WHRC would be able to develop commercial property for rent or sale to deliver corporate plan objectives. The council commissioned Savills to assess whether there was a viable business case to establish a housing company, it having been made clear in the terms of reference that the reason for setting up a company was not to compete head-to-head with large developers but to fill a gap in the market which was necessary to meet a defined need. The business plan was modelled using two typical sites within Wealden: one in the north and the other in the south and with assumptions being made as to land and property acquisition values, market rental values, construction costs, management and maintenance costs. One model only provided for the development of homes for outright sale whilst the other model retained some housing for long-term rent. Both options assumed that the proposed developments would meet planning policy affordable housing thresholds, with any affordable housing being provided through the HRA. Both business plan options provided a profit for the company but at different levels of return, it being noted that alongside any profit on the sales, a rental portfolio also provided a potential for long-term asset growth which would provide borrowing ability for future developments. The broad aims of the company were:

- to provide accommodation (for rent and sale) of a type that is not being provided by the market (and in particular flatted accommodation, bungalows, smaller unit accommodation for younger and older people and more affordable provision for retirement housing); and
- to make a profit by delivering housing for market rent or market sale with a view to providing a financial return to the council as the owner of the company.

Products to be offered by the company would be:

- housing for outright sale;
- starter homes;
- rent-to-buy;
- shared ownership;
- market rent;
- commercial regeneration opportunities.

The properties would be constructed on such council-owned land as currently exists but with the intention that the company will also purchase land on the open market including purchases 'off-plan'. Some private rented properties would accommodate future purchasers who might not yet be in a position to buy and this would be managed through a service level agreement between the company and the council – the intention being that those rented properties would meet a different need to those needs which were already being met by the private rented market or through the council's own housing stock. The company would also consider opportunities to regenerate existing properties including commercial units where it could create mixed-use sites of residential and commercial properties.

It was envisaged that the company would be funded by a mix of equity (invested by the council) and debt (borrowed either from the council or private sector lenders). The proportion of borrowing equity will be determined on a case-by-case basis. To avoid state aid issues, the company would need to be treated no more favourably than the market dictates. The proposal is for the council to lend WHRC development finance at market rates. The company would then invest a mix of debt and equity in acquiring homes and development land, securing planning consents and then constructing homes. Homes would be sold and rented for a commercial return. It is expected that the council will provide equity input to the company in the

44 Development options

initial development period to cover running costs and development costs. Over time, debts and interest will be repaid as rent income and sale receipts are secured. Where such income exceeds the company's management and maintenance costs as well as debt charges, then the profits can be used to repay further debts and eventually pay dividends to the council. It was proposed that the company will have a share capital and that the council will be the only shareholder. To avoid illegal state aid the company will be capitalised through a mixture of equity and debt financing in a ratio typically seen in private companies and housing associations. The drawdown of the equity and loan provided by the council to the company would be taken in stages as development and acquisition proposals came forward. There would be break points in the loan to enable the council to recall it if business plans or circumstances change. As with a mortgage, the interest will initially be the largest part of the loan repayment and in later years the company will repay more of the principal. In addition to the initial start-up loan, the company would also need a revolving working capital loan to support its operations during the course of its business plan. Interest on loans to the company would be recognised in the council's general fund revenue account. The principal repayments would be classified as capital receipts to the council and used to replenish the capital receipts reserve and recycled to fund other capital projects. The management of rental properties would be undertaken through a commercial contract with the council's housing service. Corporation tax is accounted for in the business plan but not any dividend distribution back to the council. Both the equity and investment loans to the company would count as capital expenditure for the purposes of the Local Government and Housing Act 1989. Regulation 25 of the Local Authorities (Capital Finance and Accounting) (England) Regulations 2003 extended the statutory definition of capital on a proper practices basis to include the giving of any loan, grant or other financial assistance to any person, whether for use by that person or third party towards expenditure or which would, if incurred by the local authority, be capital expenditure. The working capital loan, so long as it was used for day-to-day revenue purposes, would not count as capital expenditure. The requirement for the council to prepare group accounts once the company started to trade would cause additional administration for the council's finance team to consolidate and report the financial results of the company into the council's accounts. The company would need to provide information for group consolidation and have its accounts audited so as to allow the council to publish audited accounts by 31st July of each year in accordance with the Accounts and Audit Regulations 2015. Solicitors Trowers and Hamlin provided the council with legal advice relating to the setting up of the company using powers provided by section 1 Localism Act 2011.

Development options 45

On 19th October 2016 a worked-up report for the establishment of the new housing company was brought back to Wealden's Cabinet with the following officer recommendations:

- approval to the setting up of a wholly owned local authority housing and regeneration company;
- a recommended governance structure of three elected members and two officers, with responsibility for the actual appointments being delegated to the Director of Governance and Corporate Services in consultation with the Leader;
- an initial investment of £100,000 to provide working capital with further investments in line with the business plan, capital programme and state aid rules;
- a recommendation that full council amends the capital programme by viring £100,000 from the infrastructure budget;
- noting the appointment of the Director of Governance and Corporate Services to carry out the shareholder duties to include annual reporting to the audit and finance committee;
- that the council indemnifies and insures council officers and elected members who will sit on the company's board of directors.

On 15th December 2016 Wealden's housing and regeneration company was formally incorporated under the name of Sussex Weald Homes Limited (Company Number 10528563) with its registered office at Council Offices, Vicarage Lane, Hailsham B27 2AX and with a share capital of £100,000. The advantages of a local authority building new housing through an intermediary company instead of directly through its HRA include:

- the development is freed from the financial constraints of the HRA;
- it can include development for outright sale as well as social rent;
- the company can raise finance on the open market;
- although the company is constitutionally separate from its controlling local authority, the council still retains control through its shareholding;
- any rented social housing which the company develops will (unless the law changes) be kept permanently available to meet housing need as it will not be subject to right to buy;
- the ability to let on assured shortholds means that the company can (theoretically) terminate a tenancy at any time on as little as two months' statutory notice;
- any financial surplus which the company earns from its portfolio can be paid as dividends back to the council.

46 *Development options*

There is also nothing to prevent a local authority-controlled housing company seeking registered provider status with the Homes and Communities Agency. Loddon Homes (established by Wokingham Borough Council) was the first local authority-controlled housing company to achieve status as a for-profit registered provider with the HCA. That company is itself a subsidiary of Wokingham Housing Limited (which is also a council-controlled company). Having registered provider status confers additional flexibility to meet housing needs and means that the company's activities are governed by HCA standards. The main difficulty in a local authority choosing to go it alone, whether through its HRA or through an intermediary company, is that it is venturing into uncharted territory. Yes – there maybe examples of other council-controlled companies working successfully. But the issue with the council going it alone is that is retains 100% of the commercial risk without necessarily the commercial experience which is required to manage that risk. A council's core business (and the reason for its being) is the delivery of public services (including housing). And whilst recent legislation has given councils wide powers to set up companies to trade commercially, those powers can be still viewed as incidental to its public functions. There is the risk that what is commercially necessary may not always dovetail with the political preferences of the members in charge. This is why the third option for housing regeneration involves a joint venture between a local housing authority and private sector partners.

An example of this third option is the establishment of Gateshead Regeneration LLP (incorporated 29th March 2012) as a partnership between Gateshead Council and Evolution Gateshead Developments LLP (which is itself a consortium between Galliford Try Construction Limited and Home Group Developments Limited). The partnership brings together the expertise and resources of a statutory corporation, a major housebuilder and a registered housing provider. In the business review forming part of Evolution Gateshead Development LLP's 31st March 2016 members' report and financial statements, its principal activities are stated to be, *'to provide project management services and loan funding to Gateshead Regeneration LLP to enable the development of 2,400 mixed tenure housing within the Gateshead Borough over a 15–20 year period'*. The partnership was formed in March 2012 and the first bundle of sites to be constructed commenced in March 2014, with the first properties being completed and sold in March 2015. This has continued into the current financial year with properties being completed and sold in Birtley and Saltwell.

In many cases it will be considered more cost effective and financially efficient for a prospective development site to be transferred by the local authority to its development partner as vacant land and buildings, leaving it to the developer to commission and finance the carrying out of the construction itself. But there is another option. Section 2 of the Local Authorities (Land) Act 1963 permits a local authority, for the benefit or improvement of its area, to erect any building and construct or carry out works on any land. For the same purpose, section 3 of the same Act enables a local authority to advance money (up to 90% of land value) to another party to acquire land or erect any building or carry out work on that land. Any such advance must be secured by mortgage and repayable within a 30-year term. Section 4 enables a local authority to advance up to 75% to another party which enters into a building agreement with the local authority whereby that other party will enter onto land belonging to the local authority for the purpose of constructing buildings with a view to ownership of the built-out development being transferred to the developer on the completion of construction. Section 5 is a stand-alone power enabling a local authority to construct and manage off-street garaging and hard standings for the parking of motor vehicles and to let out the use of such parking provision on such terms as it considers appropriate.

5 Compulsory purchase

An advantage which local authorities have over private developers is their ability to use statutory tools to assemble land for redevelopment and to override third-party rights by converting them into a right to compensation. It is also what a local authority brings to the table in any development partnership. The key statutory tool is its power of compulsory purchase. We have already seen in Chapter 3 examples of the many powers of compulsory purchase which exist in housing and planning legislation as well as the Local Government Act 1972. However whatever statutory power is used, the *process* of compulsory purchase is spread across the following statutory provisions:

- Land Compensation Act 1961;
- Compulsory Purchase Act 1965;
- Land Compensation Act 1973;
- Acquisition of Land Act 1981;
- General Vesting Declaration Act 1981.

The legislation is to be read together with a raft of subsidiary legislation and government policy. On 29th October 2015 the DCLG published its 139-page guidance document *Compulsory Purchase Process and the Crichel Down Rules* to help councils through the compulsory purchase process. The guidance updated and replaced similar guidance issued in 2004. We shall refer to it as 'the 2015 Guidance'. Paragraph 12 on page 11 of the 2015 Guidance states under the heading 'Justifying a Compulsory Purchase Order' that *'A compulsory purchase order should only be made where there is a compelling case in the public interest. An acquiring authority should be sure that the purposes for which the compulsory purchase order is made justify interfering with the human rights of those with an interest in the land affected. Particular consideration should be given to the provisions of **Article 1 of the First Protocol to the European Convention on Human Rights** and, in* *the case of a dwelling, to **Article 8 of the Convention**.'* The essential steps towards the making and implementation of a typical compulsory purchase order can be summarised in the following steps:

- **Choosing the most appropriate statutory acquisition power.** Official guidance states that the power used should be that which is closest to the purpose for which the land is being acquired. It would therefore be expected that land required specifically for the construction of a public road would be acquired under section 239 Highways Act 1980 in preference to section 226 Town and Country Planning Act 1990. Although, as will be seen later in this chapter, there may be other advantages in making the acquisition under section 226.
- **Obtaining a valid council resolution authorising the making of the compulsory purchase order.** It means firstly identifying from the council's published constitution exactly which group of councillors is empowered to authorise the making of the CPO and then presenting a report which presents to those councillors everything they need to know to make an informed decision on every material issue relevant to the proposed CPO. That report and the resolution resulting from it are the first critical documents in the CPO process. That report will need to include a scale plan identifying the whole of the land to be covered by the CPO. There should also be presented with that report a detailed statement of reasons justifying the making of the CPO. A statement of reasons is a non-statutory document but one which the Secretary of State will require to see to before deciding whether to confirm a CPO, even one which is unopposed. Later in this chapter we examine the contents of a typical CPO report and statement of reasons.
- **Commissioning a land referencing exercise to identify all land ownerships and interests which will be affected by the CPO.** Such referencing exercise is essential where there are multiple land ownerships and interests, each of which will need to be engaged within the CPO process. However, land referencing may not be necessary where the proposed CPO will only affect a single land ownership or a small easily identifiable group of ownerships and interests. Even when a local authority is dealing with its CPO in house, a major land-referencing exercise can be more cost-effectively outsourced to a specialist land referencing organisation such as Terraquest. Land referencing is not just about examining registered title information but also includes the service of statutory questionnaires on every person known or reputed to own or occupy property within the area of the proposed CPO. Section 16 Local Government (Miscellaneous Provisions) Act 1976 allows a local authority to serve notice on any owner-occupier leaseholder,

mortgagee or person managing the property, requiring them to provide formal disclosure of their interest in the land and the name and address of the person whom they believe to be in occupation and who is otherwise interested in the land. Failure to respond to a section 16 notice is a criminal offence. The reason for serving section 16 notices is that Land Registry records do not always provide a complete and up-to-date record of land interests. Even where title to land is registered, there may be several interests (including leases of less than seven years) which do not feature on the title register because there is no legal requirement for them to do so. And more than 118 years after compulsory land registration was first introduced in London there all still many thousands of titles across England and Wales which remain unregistered simply because ownership has never changed hands. Having examined title registers, served notices, followed up and recorded responses, the referencing company will present the results back to the commissioning authority in the form of a schedule and an order map in a format compliant with the requirements of the Secretary of State (as confirming authority) and which identifies the location of each of the scheduled interests. That schedule and the accompanying order map will later be incorporated into and form part of the compulsory purchase order itself.

- **Drafting the order.** Once the land referencing is complete, the order itself can be drafted. That document may not be more than two pages long (excluding the land referencing schedule). However, it must accord to the template prescribed by the Compulsory Purchase of Land (Prescribed Forms) (Ministers) Regulations 2004 as amended. To help local authorities produce compliant CPOs, the DCLG offer an informal, free checking service, although all that the DCLG can do at this stage is to check the format of the draft CPO and the proposed order map in terms of regulatory compliance. Any typos or inconsistencies will be picked up, as will any issues relating to the scale, colourings or annotations of the proposed order map. But the DCLG will not at this stage venture any opinion on the statement of reasons or on anything else related to the justification for making the order. The purpose of this optional preliminary check is to avoid the need for the DCLG to reject a badly drawn CPO at a later (and more expensive) stage of the process purely because of a technical defect.
- **Making the compulsory purchase order.** A CPO is 'made' at the point at which it (and the order map) are executed under the common seal of the local authority and dated. Even though the 'compulsion' aspects of a CPO cannot become effective until it is confirmed by the Secretary of State, the unconfirmed CPO still has legal status. From the moment it is made, the unconfirmed CPO is registerable as a local land

charge against the property, which means that anyone dealing with the property will be alerted to its existence. There is nothing to prevent a voluntary transfer of land being made pursuant to an unconfirmed CPO and the interested party will, in most cases, receive the same statutory compensatory add-ons as if they had waited for the order to be confirmed. A voluntary acquisition made pursuant to an unconfirmed CPO will still trigger the same stamp duty land tax exemptions as if it had been made to a confirmed order.

- **Publicising the CPO.** Section 11 of the Acquisition of Land Act 1981 requires that the making of a compulsory purchase order be advertised (in the statutory format) for two successive weeks in the local press. At the same time, section 12 requires formal notice of the making of the order to be served on everybody who has a scheduled interest in the land to which it affects. It is recommended good practice that service of the statutory notice is synchronised to take place on the same date that the first statutory advertisement appears. This is because the 21-day deadline for receipt of objections to the CPO will begin on the date that first statutory advertisement appears. Enclosed with each statutory notice will normally be a copy of the CPO (as executed) as well as a copy of the executed and dated order map. The remaining enclosure is a copy of the statement of reasons. At the point the first advertisement appears or statutory notice is delivered, a copy of the executed CPO and order map must be placed on deposit at a convenient public location for public inspection. Although good practice dictates that copies of those documents will have already been sent to those affected, there may be other people seeing the advertisement who would not have previously received that information. It is also the point at which a copy of the order and map should be sent to the Registrar of Local Land Charges.
- **Applying for confirmation.** It is important that as soon as possible after the CPO has been made and advertised, formal application is made to the DCLG for its confirmation. Doing this sooner rather than later will ensure that the DCLG are fully alerted to the making of the CPO by the time the first of the objections begin to trickle in. The application for confirmation must include the non-statutory checklist (or general certificate) prescribed in section 12 of the 2015 Guidance to reassure the DCLG that there has been compliance with regulatory formalities.
- **If no objections are received.** The Secretary of State can proceed to confirm the order – or alternatively authorise the acquiring local authority to self-confirm their order. Either way, once the order has been confirmed, notice of that confirmation will need to be advertised and notices sent out in the same was that the making of the CPO was first publicised.

52 *Compulsory purchase*

- **When objections are received.** Anyone can object to the making of a CPO. That is why it is advertised. But only those objectors who have a scheduled interest are 'statutory objectors'. A CPO cannot be confirmed until any outstanding statutory objections have either been withdrawn or overruled by the Secretary of State. However, at this stage, objections will only be taken into account to the extent that they relate to the principle of compulsory purchase, not to issues of compensation. The latter are issues for the Upper Tribunal (Lands Chamber) (formerly and still commonly referred to as the Lands Tribunal) and not the Secretary of State. The DCLG will therefore routinely reject letters of objection which relate purely to monetary issues. The DCLG will notify the acquiring authority of objections received. Though in some cases those objection letters will have been addressed directly to the local authority, in which case it is the acquiring authority which will forward the objection letter to the DCLG. Receipt of statutory objections also means that the DCLG will have to determine its choice of procedure for giving the local authority and each objector a fair opportunity to present their cases for and against the confirmation of the CPO. Unless all parties are agreeable to the issues being dealt with on the basis of written representations, it will mean the DCLG issuing directions for a public inquiry into the CPO.
- **Whether the decision to confirm or not confirm a CPO will be made following a public inquiry or on the basis of written representations**, the local authority will be issued with a strict timetable for preparing and serving its statement of case on each objector with accompanying documentation (six weeks from the issue of the directions) and further milestones. Preparing for a major public inquiry is a massive and expensive task for a local authority involving service of documents on multiple parties. The inquiry procedure itself is set out in the Compulsory Purchase (Inquiry Procedure) Rules 2007.
- **Whilst preparing for a public inquiry**, the local authority must as a parallel exercise try to resolve as many the objections as possible with a view to getting them withdrawn. Negotiating away the bulk of the objections before the public inquiry takes place can be key to a successful outcome. In short, the fewer objections making it to inquiry, the stronger the council's case becomes. It means that instead of facing an entrenched campaign of opposition, the council can focus instead on that tiny hard core of objectors who refuse any compromise. Whilst an inquiry inspector will refuse to consider compensatory issues at a public inquiry, such financial issues will be at the forefront of the local authority's mind when trying to negotiate objections away. It is a bargaining shop. A problem often faced by the owners of properties

affected by a CPO is that the statutory compensation they are likely to receive for their soon-to-be-demolished property will be insufficient for them to purchase like-for-like elsewhere. It means that the local authority may have to offer enhanced compensation packages to bridge that gap. Such enhanced packages may be well worthwhile if it means that the local authority can avoid the cost, delay and uncertainty of a public inquiry.

- **Once a CPO has been confirmed by the Secretary of State** and that confirmation has been publicised as required by statute, the process of transferring title from the original owners to the acquiring authority can begin. One of the purposes of statutory advertisement is to trigger a six-week time limit for any judicial challenge to the procedures adopted.
- **There are two alternative ways in which a local authority can achieve a transfer of title from the original owner to itself.** The traditional way of doing this involves service of notice to treat inviting the owner to engage with the local authority to agree the terms of sale. The owner will have 21 days from receipt of the notice to put forward details of their compensation claim, which will then trigger a process of negotiation between that owner and the acquiring authority, leading to a transfer of title from that owner to the local authority. At the same time as serving notice to treat the local authority can at the same time serve notice of entry giving it the right to take vacant possession of the property. Whilst notice of entry will enable the local authority to take control of the property, it will not yet have title to the property. If the owner fails to respond to a notice to treat or if, following such notice, the parties are unable to agree terms, either party can make reference to the Upper Tribunal (Lands Chamber) to decide the terms of transfer. There is a separate procedure for dealing with untraced owners, which involves direct reference to the Upper Tribunal by the acquiring authority. Once the Upper Tribunal has made its determination as to the amount of compensation payable – and if the former owner still refuses to convey – the local authority can pay the assessed compensation into court and then execute a unilateral deed poll transferring title from the former owner to itself.
- **The alternative and more modern way for a local authority to obtain title to property subject to a confirmed CPO is via a general vesting declaration (GVD).** The procedure is governed by the General Vesting Declarations Act 1981 as amended. The process does not involve any formal conveyancing transaction. Instead, the acquiring authority issues a single declaration covering all the properties to which the CPO relates. On the date the GVD takes effect, unencumbered title to all those properties is deemed to have been transferred to the acquiring

authority, which may then apply to the Land Registry to substitute its name as the registered owner. The rights of the former owners and any other third-party interests are then converted into a right to compensation. Whether the acquiring authority chooses to proceed by way of a notice to treat or via a GVD, its right to implement the CPO will lapse if the acquiring authority does not begin the process of transferring title within three years from the date notice of confirmation was first advertised.

The Land Compensation Acts of 1961 and 1973 (as amended) set up the statutory framework for compensating land owners and other interested parties whose interests have been acquired under compulsory purchase. The costs of making and implementing a compulsory purchase order is generally made up of the following basic elements:

- the values of the individual properties and associated interests being acquired on the date the acquiring authority takes possession of the property or completes the transaction if earlier;
- a 10% supplement in the form of a statutory home loss payment (currently capped at £61,000) to someone who has been in owner-occupation for at least 12 months before the acquiring authority took possession;
- a 7.5% basic loss payment (currently capped at £75,000) to someone who has owned the property for more than 12 months but who has not occupied it as their main residence, such as a buy-to-let landlord;
- a disturbance payment intended to reimburse the former owner for all of their out-of-pocket expenses occasioned as a result of the implementation of the CPO as regards the purchase of their property by the acquiring authority. These will include conveyancing costs, not only in respect of the property being compulsory purchased, but also as regards any replacement property which is being acquired by the former owner. But it is not just conveyancing costs. It is likely that there will also be a substantial stamp duty land tax bill to be paid on the acquisition of the replacement property, which the acquiring authority will be required to meet. The former owner will also require reimbursement of valuation fees and other professional fees related to the owner's negotiation with the acquiring authority on a settlement figure. A disturbance payment will also cover removal costs and other expenses routinely associated with a house move.
- the acquiring authority's own conveyancing costs for each individual property acquired – which may also include stamp duty land tax save to the extent that any SDLT exemption can be claimed;

- all costs associated with the making of the CPO and (if necessary) in taking it to inquiry. In all cases this will include the internal costs and expenses in obtaining constitutional authorisation for making the CPO, as well as land referencing, statutory advertising and/or administrative work consequent on dealing with multiple parties.

Where the development is a joint venture between a local authority and a private sector development partner, it is likely that the costs of the compulsory purchase will be met by that development partner as a project cost. The acquiring authority then exercises its statutory powers on behalf the development partner and itself. If a CPO goes to a public inquiry, the general presumption under Department of the Environment Circular 8/93 is that the acquiring authority and each of the objectors will each bear their own costs in presenting their cases. However, this costs presumption assumes a successful outcome for the local authority: namely that the compulsory purchase is confirmed. The cost of failure is that the local authority must not only bear its own costs but also pay the costs of those other parties who have succeeded in their objections. Likewise, if the CPO is unilaterally withdrawn by the local authority before it even gets to public inquiry, the council will pick up the objectors' abortive costs in preparing for the inquiry up to the date of such withdrawal.

A well-drafted statement of reasons is key to the making of a successful CPO. It pulls together in one document everything which is relevant to the council's decision to make and pursue a CPO. In many respects the information contained in the statement of reasons overlaps what is contained in that other critical initiating document: the Cabinet Report (see below). But a statement of reasons is more than just a compliance document: it must also convince. Section 11 paragraph 154 of the 215 Guidance states that the information contained in the statement of reasons should include:

- a brief description of the order land and its location, topographical features and present use;
- an explanation of the use of the particular enabling power;
- an outline of the authority's purpose in seeking to acquire the land;
- a statement of the authority's justification for compulsory purchase with regard to Article 1 of the First Protocol to the European Convention on Human Rights and Article 8 if appropriate;
- a description of the proposals for the use or development of the land;
- a statement about the planning position of the order site;
- specific information required by government policy statements where the relevant circumstances apply;

56 Compulsory purchase

- any special considerations affecting the site, for example: ancient monuments; listed buildings; conservation areas; special category land, consecrated land, renewal area etc;
- if the mining code has been included, reasons for doing so;
- details of how the acquiring authority seeks to overcome any obstacle for which prior consent is needed before the order scheme can be implemented (for example a waste management licence);
- details of any views which may have been expressed by a government department about the proposed development of the order site;
- what steps the authority has taken to negotiate for the acquisition of the land by agreement;
- other information which would be of interest to persons affected by the order (such as proposals to rehouse displaced residents or relocate businesses);
- details of any related order, application or appeal which may require a co-ordinated decision by a confirming minister (such as a planning appeal, road closure or listed building);
- a list of any documents which the acquiring authority intend to present to any public inquiry including maps or plans, together with details of where those documents can be inspected.

In Chapter 1 we touched on the statement of reasons used by Camden Council to justify its London Borough of Camden (Part of Agar Grove Estate) Compulsory Purchase Order 2015. We now look in more details at the structure at that document. The document itself can be freely downloaded from the internet. What follows is a summary of this 29-page document. The contents comprise:

- an introductory summary of the proposal;
- a background and description of the order land. Although the council already owned the entirety of the freehold, what it needed to re-acquire under the CPO are those remaining flat leases which had previously been sold off under right-to-buy and not already repurchased;
- project background and purpose of using CPO. Reference is made to extensive consultations with existing residents and how the council responded to those consultations. It explains what the scheme (as a whole) will deliver as regards new homes and associated facilities, including communal and commercial facilities and transport improvements
- how the construction work will be phased and what arrangements will be put in place to re-house existing tenants. Leaseholders whose

interests were being repurchased were offered the following three options:

(i) A cash purchase of the leasehold interest at open market value plus 10% Home loss (capped at £49,000) for resident owners or 7.5% basic loss (capped at £75,000) for non-resident owners – together with reimbursement of other costs and expenses.

(ii) A shared equity replacement property, where the leaseholder buys a given equity share (for example 75%) and with the council owning the remaining share. However, unlike shared ownership, the leaseholder would not pay rent on the council's share. The offer of a shared equity would be conditional on a detailed assessment of the leaseholder's financial circumstances, to ensure that individual leaseholders are investing the maximum they can afford without hardship. Those leaseholders who do not meet this threshold would instead be offered shared ownership (part own/part rent) as an alternative.

(iii) The option for leaseholders unable to purchase another property is to become social housing tenants, either in this regeneration scheme or in another part of the borough – but only where the leaseholder is experiencing severe hardship. Those leaseholders would still be offered 25% of the full property value to facilitate the swap to tenancy (as set out in the *DCLG Stock Valuation Guide*).

- an explanation of the statutory power used by Camden Council to make the CPO: which in this case was section 226 Town and Country Planning Act 1990 and the issues which the Secretary of State will take into account when deciding to grant compulsory purchase powers, namely:

    (i) whether the purpose for which the land is being acquired fit in with the adopted planning framework for the area or core strategy;
    (ii) the extent to which the proposed purpose will contribute to the promotion or improvement of the economic, social or environmental well-being of the area;
    (iii) potential financial viability of the scheme for which the land is being acquired;
    (iv) whether the purpose for which the authority is proposing to acquire the land could be achieved by other means;

- explanation that the council's development control committee had resolved to grant planning permission on 3rd April 2014, with the final planning permission having been issued on 4th August 2014 (under reference 2013/8088/P) and that the order accords with Camden plan objectives to: develop new solutions with partners to reduce inequality;

create conditions for and harness the benefits of economic growth; invest in communities to ensure sustainable neighbourhoods; deliver value for money services through inclusive residents' consultation and commitment to quality. This section also puts the proposal in context of the National Planning Policy Framework; the London Plan; local planning policy as well as Camden's Housing Strategy 2011–2016;

- that no part of the order land is within a conservation area and does not include any listed buildings or scheduled ancient monuments. That no part of the order land comprises greenbelt, metropolitan open space, common land or other public open space;
- states that the council has selected a contractor in accordance with EU Procurement Rules; that the council will fund the project from its own resources and borrowing; and has the necessary internal authorities to proceed with the order subject to its confirmation by the Secretary of State;
- the statement also contains the critical human rights and equalities paragraphs demonstrating (in detail) the extent to which Camden Council had regard to its statutory responsibilities under the European Human Rights Convention and the Equality Act 2010, and its need to demonstrate that its use of compulsory purchase powers was in the public interest and proportionate to the ends being pursued.
- the statement of reasons concludes with a list of every document which the council would intend to refer to or put in evidence at a public inquiry.

However, the initiating document in any compulsory purchase process is the officer report to the specific group of councillors with the power to authorise the making of that CPO. That group of councillors could be the Cabinet or a named committee of the council or at a meeting of full council. The starting point is to identify from the council's published constitution to whom the report should be presented. In many respects the content of that officer report will mirror the information contained in the statement of reasons. But the underlying purpose of that report and the consequent resolution is to ensure that council officers have all the authority they need to make a CPO; publicise it; apply for Secretary of State confirmation; take it to inquiry, and implement it (if confirmed). Officers will also need authorisation to enter into negotiations directly with those affected by the CPO with a view to agreeing terms for voluntary purchase. Westminster Council's 14th December 2015 Cabinet report relating to a proposed compulsory purchase order for the redevelopment of its Ebury Bridge Estate provides an example of what such an initiating report should contain. We focus on the recommendations of that report, which can be summarised as follows:

- That the Cabinet agree to the making of a compulsory purchase order under sections 226 and 227 Town and Country Planning Act 1990 (as amended); sections 13 and 15 Local Government (Miscellaneous Provisions) Act 1976 in accordance with the procedures in the Acquisition of Land Act 1981 and to create new rights facilitating the development (and refurbishment of part) of the Ebury Bridge Estate, as defined by the CPO red line plan and other relevant powers to acquire all outstanding land and interests within the red line plan of the site.

- The Cabinet delegate power to the Executive Director of Growth, Planning and Housing (EDGPH) authority in consultation with the Director of Law to approve the statement of reasons, the order map (for which the plan attached to the report was only indicative), and the order schedule and any other supporting documentation as is necessary to finalise before submission, to commence the CPO process and effect any other procedural requirements including (but not limited to) the publication and service of all notices and the presentation of the council's case in the event of a public inquiry.
- That Cabinet delegates power to the EDGPH to acquire any interests in land within the order area by agreement and the making of payments equivalent to statutory compensation or additional payments as shall be deemed reasonable in the circumstances and the provision of property or services in lieu of compensation in consultation with the Director of Law in contemplation of the order being made.
- That the Cabinet delegate power to the EDGPH working with the Director of Law in consultation with the Cabinet members to ensure that, if the CPO is confirmed, it is implemented and to take all necessary steps to implement these recommendations, finalising the terms of the proposed arrangements in accordance with the terms set out in this report.
- That if the CPO is confirmed, power is delegated to the EDGPH to settle the compensation amounts to acquire such interests where voluntary agreement cannot be reached;
- That's the Cabinet authorise officers to take all necessary steps to implement these recommendations.

As an initiating report is likely to contain sensitive as well as non-sensitive information, any parts of the report which identify private individuals or relate to financial negotiations must be classified as 'exempt' and kept out of the public domain.

From the date of the initiating resolution, through to the making of the CPO and up to the start of any public inquiry, the local authority is in a race to complete as many voluntary transactions as is possible to reduce or eliminate outstanding objections to the CPO process. Once the last objection has been withdrawn, the scheduled public inquiry can be cancelled and the order confirmed. Whilst compensation is not an issue for the Secretary of State, it is certainly an issue for property owners and councils trying to negotiate

60 Compulsory purchase

with them. A common problem when right to buy leases are being repurchased to facilitate redevelopment is that (even with the statutory supplements) the amounts that those owners are likely to receive for their interests will still fall well short from the cash they need to purchase another property in which to relocate. We have already seen how Camden Council sought to address this through its offer to leaseholds of a replacement shared equity property or reversion from leasehold status to that of a secure tenant supplemented by a payment equivalent to 25% of property value to assist with the transition. However, those former leaseholders will still be worse off in that none of them would own their new home outright.

Where the financial difference between the value of the repurchased interest and the cost to the affected party of buying a new home is manageable, a local authority can (at its discretion) provide further financial top-up assistance to the displaced freeholder or leaseholder under the Regulatory Reform (Housing Assistance) (England and Wales) Order 2002, the relevant provisions of which are set out below:

3. Power of Local Housing Authorities to Provide Assistance

(1) For the purpose of improving living conditions in their area, a local housing authority may provide directly or indirectly assistance to any person for the purpose of enabling him –

(a) to acquire living accommodation (whether inside or outside their area);

(b) to adapt or improve living accommodation (whether by alteration, conversion or enlargement by the installation of anything or injection of any substance or otherwise);

(c) to repair living accommodation;

(d) to demolish buildings comprising or including living accommodation;

(e) where buildings comprising or including living accommodation have been demolished, to construct buildings that comprise or include replacement living accommodation.

(2) The power conferred by paragraph (1)(a) may be exercised to assist a person to acquire living accommodation only where the authority –

(a) have acquired or proposed to acquire (whether compulsorily or otherwise) his existing living accommodation; or

(b) are satisfied that the acquisition of other living accommodation would provide for that person a benefit similar to that which would be provided by the carrying out of work of any description in relation to his existing living accommodation.

Compulsory purchase 61

(3) *Assistance may be provided in any form.*
(4) *Assistance may be unconditional or subject to conditions, including conditions as to the repayment of the assistance or of its value (in whole or in part), or the making of a contribution towards the assisted work; but before imposing any such condition, or taking steps to enforce it, a local housing authority shall have regard to the ability of the person concerned to make that repayment or contribution.*
(5) *Before a local housing authority provide assistance to any person, they shall –*

    (a) give to that person a statement in writing of the conditions (if any) to which the assistance is to be subject; and
    (b) satisfy themselves that the person has received appropriate advice or information about the extent and nature of any obligation (whether financial or otherwise) to which he will become subject in consequence of the provision of assistance.

(6) *A local housing authority may take any form of security in respect of the whole or part of any assistance.*
(7) *Where any such security is taken in the form of a charge on any property the local housing authority may at an time reduce the priority of the charge or secure its removal.*
(8) *This article is subject to articles 4 and 5.*
(9) *Nothing in this article affects any power of a local housing authority under Part 14 of the 1985 Act (loans for acquisition or improvement of housing).*

4. Provision of assistance: supplementary

A local housing authority may not exercise the power conferred by Article 3 in any case unless –

    (a) they have adopted a policy for the provision of assistance under that article;
    (b) they have given public notice of the adoption of the policy;
    (c) they have secured that –

        (i) a document in which the policy is set out in full is available for inspection, free of charge, at their principal office at all reasonable times; and
        (ii) copies of a document containing a summary of the policy may be obtained by post (on payment, where a reasonable charge is made, of the amount of the charge); and

    (d) the power is exercised in that case in accordance with that policy.

The cost to local authorities of making any financial tops-up under the 2002 Order must be balanced against the savings in time and money if the local authority and any development partner can get on with the project without having to await the outcome (and uncertainties) of a public inquiry. When notice of a compulsory purchase order is advertised, it is not unusual to receive objections from public utilities (such as electricity companies or telecommunications operators). Such objections are routinely lodged to protect the interests of the utility company and will be withdrawn once a documented arrangement has been put in place to secure their interest.

Once the CPO has been made advertised and when the last objection has been received, the next milestone for the local authority is the publication of its statement of case as required by the Compulsory Purchase (Inquiries Procedure) Rules 2007.

Rule 7 requires an acquiring authority, within six weeks of the relevant date, to send a statement of case to each remaining objector and to the Secretary of State. Unless that statement of case is accompanied by copies of all documentation which the acquiring authority intends to use at the inquiry, the acquiring authority must also specify a place (within reasonable distance of the land being acquired) at which that documentation can be inspected free of charge and at all reasonable hours. That documentation must remain on deposit and available for public inspection up to the start of the public inquiry. The relevant date will be specified in the opening letter from the Secretary of State announcing the intention to convene a public inquiry and is the official start date of that process. At that point and following receipt of objections it is likely that counsel would have already been appointed to represent the local authority at the forthcoming inquiry and it is that counsel who will usually have the last word as to what goes in the acquiring authority's statement of case.

In many respects the statement of case will repeat information already provided in the earlier statement of reasons justifying the making of the CPO. But it is also likely that by the time that statement of the case is issued matters will have moved on and that there will be additional issues to address in the document arising from matters raised in the letters of objection, which will need to be answered in the statement of case. Rule 7 also gives the Secretary of State discretion to issue notice requiring an objector to provide a statement of their own within six weeks from notice requiring them to do so.

Rule 15 deals with the presentation of evidence at the inquiry itself. It is permissible for a person giving evidence at a public inquiry to read their evidence from a written proof of evidence. A copy of that proof of evidence and a summary (if more than 1,500 words) must have been given to the appointed inspector and to each remaining objector at least three weeks before the start of the inquiry.

6 Other statutory tools

Although there are many statutory provisions authorising a local authority to compulsory purchase land for different public functions, it would seem that for most housing regeneration projects there is preference for section 226 Town and Country Planning Act 1990. There is a good reason for this. Acquisition under section 226 engages what is now section 204 Housing and Planning Act 2016. In the Chapter 2 of this book (Information Gathering) we looked at the various third-party rights and interests which can affect any title to land. This can include: restrictive covenants; private rights of way; pipes, wires, cables, and other rights over the land benefiting adjoining owners or leaseholders. The larger the registered title the more rights are likely to be registered against it, perhaps running into several pages. In some cases, the route of a right of way or service easement will be marked on the title plan which accompanies the register of title. But more often grants or reservations of service easements are expressed on the title in general terms: meaning that the routes of some services have to be identified through other means, such as: utility searches, inspections or ground surveys. Another issue is that not all third-party rights may even appear on the title register. Some third-party rights are classed in land law as 'overriding', which means that they affect a registered title even though there is no mention made of those rights or interests on any document. Overriding rights include: the rights of persons in actual occupation of property and easements acquired through long user (which under the Prescription Act 1832 can be for as little as 20 years). Such prescriptive easements can include rights of light.

Unless there is a statutory means of overriding such third-party rights and interests by converting them into a right to compensation, many regeneration projects could not take place because the land would be sterilised. For private developers, the only way to overcome onerous third-party rights is: by trying to negotiate them away; (in the case of restrictive covenants) by an application to the Upper Tribunal (Lands Chamber) under section 84 Law of Property Act 1925 for an order discharging or modifying them on the grounds of obsolescence or because they impede some reasonable use of land for which planning permission has been obtained; or (where the third rights are no longer considered enforceable) by purchasing single premium title indemnity insurance. For local authorities there is a quicker way of overcoming third-party rights: by acquiring or appropriating the land from its existing statutory purpose to planning purposes.

Under the heading 'Power to override easements and other rights', Section 203 Housing and Planning Act 2016 (which replaced section 237 Town and Country Planning Act 1990) states:

(1) *a person may carry out building or maintenance work to which this subsection applies even if it involves –*

    (a) *Interfering with a relevant right or interest, or*
    (b) *breaching a restriction as to the user of land arising by virtue of a contract.*

(2) *subsection (1) applies to building or maintenance work where –*

    (a) *there is a planning consent for the building or maintenance work,*
    (b) *the work is carried out on land that has at any time on or after the date on with this section comes into force –*

        (i) *become vested in or acquired by a specified authority, or*
        (ii) *been appropriated by a local authority for planning purposes as defined by Section 246(1) of the Town and Country Planning Act 1990,*

    (c) *the authority could acquire the land compulsorily for the purposes of the building or maintenance work, and*
    (d) *The building or maintenance work is for purposes related to the purposes for which land was vested, acquired or appropriated as mentioned in paragraph (b)*

(3) *Subsection (1) also applies to building or maintenance work where –*

    (a) *there is planning consent for the building or maintenance work,*
    (b) *the work is carried out on other qualifying land,*
    (c) *the qualifying authority in relation to the land could acquire the land compulsorily for the purposes of the building or maintenance work, and*
    (d) *the building or maintenance work is for purposes related to the purposes for which the land was vested in or acquired or appropriated by the qualifying authority in relation to the land.*

(4) A person may use land in a case to which this subsection applies even if the use involves-

(a) interfering with a relevant right or interest, or
(b) breaching a restriction as to the user of land or arising by virtue of a contract.

The remaining subsections are consequential. But note in particular that section 204 cannot override the rights of a public utility or communications operator or any right or interest in the land which belongs to the National Trust.

To engage section 203 the following conditions must be satisfied:

- the land has at some time been acquired or appropriated by the local authority for planning purposes;
- the authority (if it had not already owned the land) would have been empowered to compulsory purchase it for the proposed building construction or other works;
- there is in place an existing planning permission for the carrying out of the building construction or other work and any associated change of use.

Where a compulsory purchase order is expressed to have been made pursuant to section 226 Town and Country Planning Act 1990, section 203 of the 2016 Act is automatically engaged on completion of the acquisition. Where the land is already owned by the local authority but for a different statutory function, a formal appropriation of that land to planning purposes is first required to engage section 203. But in either case section 203 can only apply to construction work (with or without an associated change of use) pursuant to an express grant of planning permission.

Where section 203 is engaged, any ability which the third party has to enforce that right directly (for example by obtaining an injunction) is converted instead into a right to compensation which will be assessed (if not agreed) by the Upper Tribunal. In practice it will be the exception rather than the rule that any compensation claims are actually made. And where any such claims are made, compensation will be based on proof of actual loss, not on 'ransom value'. The relevant law is set out in section 204 of the 2016 Act which states under the heading 'Compensation for overridden easements etc':

(1) a person is liable to pay compensation for any interference with a relevant right or interest or breach of a restriction that is authorised by Section 203,

(2) the compensation is to be calculated on the same basis as compensation payable under **sections 7 and 10 of the Compulsory Purchase Act 1965**.

(3) Where a person other than a specified or qualifying authority is liable to pay compensation under this section but has not paid-

    (a) the liability is enforceable against the authority, but

    (b) the authority may recover from that person any amount it pays out.

(4) The specified or qualifying authority against which a liability is enforceable by virtue of subsection (3)(a) is the specified or qualifying authority in which the land to which the compensation relates was vested, or by which the land was acquired or appropriated, as mentioned in section 203.

(5) Any dispute about compensation payable under this section may be referred to and determined by the Upper Tribunal.

Appropriating land from one statutory purpose to a different statutory purpose (with a view to engaging section 203) is a multi-stage process generally involving:

- ascertainment of the existing statutory purpose for which the land is being held and anything restricting the sale or use of that land for any other purpose (see Chapter 3 – Information Gathering);
- a formal cabinet or committee resolution authorising the appropriation of the land from one statutory function to another;
- applying for any Secretary of State consent which is required before the particular appropriation can take place (for instance under section 19 Housing Act 1985 if the land to be appropriated out of HRA includes a house or part of a house – whether or not that house is actually occupied at the date the appropriation takes place);
- compliance with any other intervening formality (such as the requirement under section 122 to advertise any intended appropriation of public open space to a different purpose (and giving consideration to any representations received pursuance to those advertisements before confirming the appropriation);
- recording the appropriation in a document containing details of: the date of the appropriation; the resolution approving it; the existing statutory purpose for which the land is held; the new statutory purpose for which the land is appropriated; the value of the land; detailing any other consent or approval authorising the appropriation;
- updating Land Registry records with the change in legal status of the land (if it is considered necessary to do so).

Other statutory tools 67

An example of a Cabinet report recommending appropriation is the 25th February 2016 report to Harlow's Cabinet recommending the appropriation of The Briars, Copshall Close and Aylets Field from housing to planning purposes to enable the existing estate of 218 bungalows to be replaced with 342 properties that include 200 affordable units as part of Harlow Council's Priority Estates Programme and pursuant to a development agreement entered into between the council and its preferred partners, Countryside Properties (UK) Ltd and Home Group Developments. The recommendations to Cabinet were:

> *(A) Cabinet agree, in principle, that the Council should exercise its statutory powers to appropriate the land at The Briars, Copshall Close and Aylets Field (BCA) for planning purposes.*
>
> *(B) Authority be delegated to the Chief Operating Officer, in consultation with the Portfolio Holders for Housing and Regeneration and Enterprise, to take all necessary actions to effect the appropriation (on a phased approach if considered appropriate)*

The stated reasons for those two recommendations were:

> *(A) The appropriation of the land for planning purposes is necessary to facilitate the redevelopment of BCA to improve the social, economic and environmental well being of the area. Without appropriation of the land for planning purposes there would be a risk that the proposed development would not be delivered.*
>
> *(B) It is considered that the public benefit of the appropriation for planning purposes is likely to outweigh any private rights which might be interfered with as a result of appropriation for planning purposes.*

The report provides legal explanation as set out in the following paragraphs:

> • *If the Council wishes to appropriate the land (or any parts of it), it will need to be satisfied that the provisions of Section 122 of The Local Government Act 1972, namely that the area of land in question is no longer required for the purposes for which it was held immediately before appropriation. The Council should also be satisfied that the relevant area of land should be appropriated such that it becomes held for planning purposes by applying the tests set out in Section 226(1) and (1A) of the Town and Country Planning Act 1990. The Council will need to consider the following factors:*
>
> > *a) Identification of the purpose for which the land is currently held.*
> > *b) Whether the land is no longer required for that purpose.*

68   *Other statutory tools*

c) Whether the appropriation will facilitate the carrying out of development, redevelopment or improvement on or in relation to the land and whether this is likely to contribute to the achievement of the economic, social or environmental wellbeing of the area

- *It should be noted that:*

  a) The land is currently being held for housing purposes, with areas of open space.

  b) The land is no longer required for this purpose on the basis that the housing and open space that exists is no longer fit for purpose in its current state and is in need of redevelopment in accordance with the planning consent that has been granted.

  c) Appropriation will facilitate the development of housing that will meet the needs of the local community and which will contribute to the achievement of the economic, social and environmental well-being of the area.

- *Under Section 122 of the Local Government Act 1972, appropriation may be made when the land is no longer needed in the public interest of the locality for the purpose for which it is held immediately before appropriation. In this regard a broad view of local need (taking account of the interests of all residents in the locality), has to be taken and officers consider that this test has been met. Officers are also satisfied that the use of appropriation would be in the public interest and proportionate to the objectives of the redevelopment scheme for the purpose of the Human Rights Act 1998. Section 122 of the Local Government Act 1972 requires that prior to appropriation the Council (in relation to the open space areas on the BCA site):*

  a) advertises its intention to do so for two consecutive weeks and
  b) considers any objections to the proposed appropriation.

The report's reference to the Human Rights Act 1998 is important because, like compulsory purchase, appropriation amounts to a confiscation of third-party rights to promote the public interest, which engages Article 1 of the First Protocol and Article 8 of the Human Rights Convention. However, what is noticeably absent from the officer report is any financial assessment of the cost of this particular appropriation. That cost should be an estimate of the statutory compensation (if any) which the council may have to pay the owners of the rights which have been appropriated. Good practice dictates that before presenting an appropriation report for approval, there should at least be an attempt to identify any third-party rights which are potentially affected so that the council is able to budget for any foreseeable compensation claims. Whether the council should actively go further by contacting those third parties and trying to negotiate away their interests is a matter of professional judgment in each case. The risk is that approaching third parties in this way may have the effect of inviting compensation claims which might not otherwise arise. It is also to be expected that such financial information would be in a part of the report which is exempt from publication.

Note also section 226 Town and Country Planning Act 1990 which states that on completion of a compulsory acquisition of land under sections 226, 228 or 230 of that Act all *private* rights of way and rights relating to the laying down, erecting, continuing or maintaining any apparatus on, under or over the land shall be extinguished and that ownership of any such apparatus shall transfer to the acquiring authority. Any person suffering loss as result of the extinguishment of their rights or ownership of their apparatus shall be entitled to compensation under the Land Compensation Act.

However, neither section 203 of the 2016 Act nor section 237 of the 1990 Act apply to public rights of way, for which other statutory provisions apply (see below), nor to third-party rights and apparatus belonging to public utilities (such as water, gas, sewerage, water or telecommunications undertakers). For the latter, the procedures set out in sections 271–272 of the 1990 Act apply.

Under the heading 'Extinguishment of rights of statutory undertakers: preliminary notices', section 271 states as follows:

> *(1) This section applies where any land has being acquired by a minister, local authority or statutory undertakers* **under Part IX of this Act or Chapter V of Part I of the Planning (Listed Buildings and Conservation Areas) Act 1990** *or compulsorily under any other enactment or has been appropriated by a local authority for planning purposes and –*
>
> *(a) there subsists over that land a right vested in or belonging to statutory undertakers for the purpose of the carrying on of their undertaking, being a right of way or a right of laying down, erecting, continuing on maintaining apparatus on, under or over land, or*
>
> *(b) there is on, under or over the land apparatus vested in or belonging to statutory undertakers for the purpose of the carrying on of their undertaking.*
>
> *(2) If the acquiring or appropriating authority is satisfied that the extinguishment of the right, or as the case maybe the removal of*

the apparatus is necessary for the purpose of carrying out any development with a view to which the land was acquired or appropriated they may serve on the statutorily undertakers a notice –

(a) stating that at the end of the relevant period the right will be extinguished; or
(b) requiring that before the end of that period the apparatus shall be removed

(3) The statutory undertakers on whom a notice is served under subsection (2) may before the end of 28 days from the date of service of the notice, serve a counternotice notice on the acquiring or appropriating authority –

(a) stating that they all object to or any of the provisions of the notice, and
(b) specifying the grounds of the objection.

(4) If no counternotice is served under subsection (3) –

(a) any right to which the notice relates shall be extinguished at the end of the relevant period; and
(b) if at the end of that period any requirement of the notice as to the removal of any apparatus has not been complied with, the acquiring or appropriating authority may remove the apparatus and dispose of it in any way the authority think fit.

(5) If a counternotice is served under subsection (3) on the local authority or on statutory undertakers, the authority or undertakers may either –

(a) withdraw the notice (without prejudice to the service of a further notice); or
(b) apply to the Secretary of State and the appropriate Minister for an order under this section embodying the provisions of the notice with or without modification

(6)–(8) [contains supplementary provisions]

Under the heading 'Extinguishment of rights of telecommunications code system operators: preliminary notices', Section 272 of the 1990 Act applies where:

(1) . . . any land has been acquired by a minister, a local authority or statutory undertakers under Part IX of this Act or under Chapter V of Part I of the (Planning Listed Buildings and Conservation

Other statutory tools 71

Areas) Act 1990 or compulsorily under any other enactment or has been appropriated by a local authority for planning purposes and –

*(a) there subsists over that land a right conferred by or in accordance with the **Electronic Communications Code on the operator of an Electronic Communications Code Network** being a right of way or a right of laying down, erecting, or continuing in maintaining apparatus on under or over the land; or*

(b) there is on, under or over the land electronic communications apparatus kept installed for the purposes of any such network.

(2) *If the acquiring or appropriating authority is satisfied that the extinguishment of the right or, as the case may be, the removal of the apparatus is necessary for the purpose of carrying out any development with a view to which the land was acquired or appropriated, they may serve on the operator of the electronic communications code network a notice –*

(a) stating that at the end of the relevant period the right will be extinguished; or

(b) requiring that before the end of that period the apparatus shall be removed.

(3) *the operator of the electronics communications code network on whom a notice is served under subsection (2) may, before the end of the period of 28 days from the date of service of the notice, serve a counter notice on the acquiring or appropriating authority –*

(a) stating that he objects to all or any of the provisions of the notice; and

(b) specifying the grounds of his objection.

(4) *If no counter notice is served under subsection (3) –*

(a) any right to which the notice relates shall be extinguished at the end of the relevant period; and

(b) If at the end of that period any requirement of the notice as to the removal of any apparatus has not been complied with, the acquiring or appropriating authority may remove the apparatus and dispose of it in anyway the authority may think fit.

(5) *If a counternotice is served under subsection (3) on a local authority or on statutory undertakers, the authority or undertakers may either –*

(a) withdraw the notice (without prejudice to the service of a further notice); or

72 *Other statutory tools*

    (b) apply to the Secretary of State and the Secretary of State for Trade and Industry for an order under this section embodying the provisions of the notice, with or without modification

(6)–(8) [contains supplementary provisions]

Section 274 deals with the making of ministerial orders under sections 271 or 272. Before making such an order the minister must first give the relevant statutory undertaker or operator of the electronic communications code network an opportunity of objecting to the proposed order. The minister must then consider any objection received and give that statutory undertaker or electronic communications code operator an opportunity of appearing before and being heard by a person appointed for that purpose by the Secretary of State and the appropriate minister. Where an order is made under section 271 or 272:

(a) any right to which the order relates shall be extinguished at the end of the period specified in the order; and
(b) if at the end of the period so specified in relation to any apparatus any requirement of the order at to the removal of the apparatus has not been complied with, the acquiring or appropriating authority may remove the apparatus and dispose of it in anyway the authority think it.

Reference to the Electronic Communications Code is to the statutory regime for telecommunications operators originally introduced by the Telecommunications Act 1984 as the 'Telecommunications Code' as extended by the Communications Act 2003 and renamed the Electronic Communications Code. The code established a regulatory regime balancing the rights of telecommunications operators and landowners as regards long-term installation and use of telecommunications apparatus. On 27th April 2017 the Digital Economy Act received Royal Assent and introduced, amongst other things, a new Electronic Communications Code.

As well as buying out the interests of right-to-buy leaseholders, a housing regeneration project is also likely to involve the displacement of existing HRA tenants. It is likely that most of those affected will have lifetime security of tenure as secure tenants under the Housing Act 1985 as well as the statutory right-to-buy. Schedule 2 of the 1985 Act lists the statutory grounds on which a county court can grant a possession order against a secure tenant. A new ground 10A was introduced by the Housing and Planning Act 1986, which states:

    The dwelling-house is in an area which is the subject of a redevelopment scheme approved by the Secretary of State or the Regulator of

Social Housing or Scottish homes in accordance with Part V of this Schedule and the landlord intends within a reasonable time of obtaining possession to dispose of the dwelling house in accordance with this scheme; or
Part of the dwelling-house is in such an area and the landlord intends within a reasonable time of taking possession to dispose of that part in accordance with the scheme and for that purpose reasonably requires possession of the dwelling house.

As regards the approval of schemes to which ground 10A will apply, Part V of Schedule 2 states (in relation to such schemes);

[summarised] *the Secretary of State may on the application of the landlord approve a scheme for the disposal and redevelopment of an area of land consisting of and including the whole or part of one or more dwelling-houses. Where a landlord proposes to apply to the Secretary of State for such approval, it shall serve written notice on any secure tenant affected by the proposal stating the main features of the scheme; that the landlord intends to apply to the Secretary of State for approval of that scheme; and the effect of such approval as regards any proceedings for possession of the dwelling-house. The secure tenant then has at least twenty eight days from receipt of the notice, to make representations to the landlord about the proposal, which the landlord is then obliged to consider before proceeding with its application to the Secretary of State. In considering whether to approve a scheme the Secretary of State must have regard to representations received and take particular account of –*

(a) the effect of the scheme on the extent and character of housing accommodation in the neighbourhood,
(b) over what period of time it is proposed that the disposal and redevelopment will take place in accordance with the scheme, and
(c) to what extent the scheme includes provision for housing provided under the scheme to be sold or let to existing tenants or persons nominated by the landlord.

Note also that the court has a discretion whether or not to grant possession of a dwelling house under ground 10A and will only do so is satisfied that suitable accommodation will be available for the displaced tenant.

Sections 138A and 138B of the Housing Act 1985 (as amended by the Housing Act 2004) allow a local authority landlord intending to carry out redevelopment to serve 'demolition notices' on those secure tenants who

74 *Other statutory tools*

are affected. The effect of a demolition notice is to temporarily suspend that tenant's right-to-buy pending the carrying out of the redevelopment. Demolition notices come in two types: an 'initial demolition notice' and a 'final demolition notice'. Schedule 5A deals with the process of serving initial demolition notices and is summarised as follows:

1. *An Initial Demolition Notice is a notice served on a secure tenant-*

    (a) stating that the landlord intends to demolish the dwellinghouse or the building within which it is contained,

    (b) setting out the reasons why the landlord intends to demolish the premises and the [reasonable] period [not exceeding seven years] within they are intended to be demolished,

    (c) stating that while the notice remains in force the landlord will not be under any obligation to transfer the property under right to buy [although this does not prevent a secure tenant pursuing a right to buy claim up to the point of completion].

2. *Subject to compliance with statutory publicity requirements, an initial demolition notice takes effect on the date it is served on the secure tenant and will remain in force for the period specified. The notice must also advise recipients of their right to claim compensation under Section 138C of the Act for abortive legal and other professional expenditure already incurred in pursuing a right to buy claim up to the point the Demolition Notice was served.*

3. *Deals with revocation or termination of Initial Demolition Notices.*

4. *Deals with the transfer of Initial Demolition Notices where a landlord's interest is transferred to another landlord.*

5. *Imposes a five year moratorium on the service of a further Initial Demolition Notice where an earlier notice has been withdrawn or has otherwise ceased to have affect without the premises having been demolished. However the Secretary of State may authorise service of the final demolition notice during that period.*

Paragraph 13(7) and (8) of Schedule 5 (which also applies to final demolition notices) requires the making of an initial demolition notice to be publicised in each of the following ways:

- by advertisement in any newspaper section circulating in the locality (other than a newspaper published by the local authority itself);
- by advertisement in any newspaper which the local authority publishes itself; and
- on the council's own website.

Any such public notice must:

- identify the property or properties affected,
- state the reasons why the demolition order has been made,
- proposed demolition date;
- the date when the demolition notice will cease to have effect;
- explain any right to compensation under section 138(C).

Compulsory purchase and the additional powers already referred to in this chapter only apply to the acquisition, appropriation or overriding of private rights and interests in land. However, a prospective regeneration site may also be affected by public rights of way which need to be closed off and extinguished to enable redevelopment to take place. Such rights of way may include made-up roads as well as footpaths. Some of those rights of way may be shown on an official highways map or (in the case of footpath or bridleways) on the 'definitive map' which the local highway authority is required by law to maintain. However, whilst an official highway map or definitive map can be regarded as conclusive evidence of the existence of a public right of way, the converse unfortunately is not true. It means that a public right of way can still exist in law even though it is not shown on any official map. Twenty years unrestricted user by the public at large is enough for the purposes of section 31 Highways Act 1980 to create a presumption that a public right of way may exist. Neither does the fact that a particular road or path is not 'adopted' by the local highway authority mean that the public right of way does not exist. As a matter of highway law, estate roads and paths fall into the following three types:

- adopted highway (where the highway authority takes direct responsibility for its maintenance and repair);
- unadopted highway, which is subject to a public right of way but where the maintenance obligation remains with the owner of the subsoil;
- private estate roads which exist only for the use of persons having the benefit of private rights of way over them.

Where no public right of way exists, any private rights can be swept up through the compulsory purchase process or by appropriation of the land to planning purposes. However, the position is different for public rights of way. In the case of many undocumented roads and footpaths, the exact highway status may be uncertain. A professional view may then need to be taken as to whether it should be treated as highway or whether it would be safe to assume that its use is entirely private. There are currently two statutory procedures for extinguishing or diverting public rights of way.

76 *Other statutory tools*

The most basic (and the oldest) is that contained section 116 Highways Act 1980, which re-enacts legislation dating back to 1835, and which states, under the heading 'Power of Magistrates Court to Authorise Stopping up or Diversion of Highway':

> *(1) Subject to the provisions of this section, if it appears to a magistrates court, after a view, if the court thinks fit, by any two or more of the justices comprising the court, that a highway (other than a trunk road or a special road) as respects which the highway authority have made an application under this section –*
>
> *(a) is unnecessary, or*
> *(b) can be diverted so as to make it nearer or more commodious to the public,*
> *the court may by order authorise it to be stopped up or as the case may be, to be so diverted.*
>
> *(2) [Repealed]*
> *(3) [Summarised] If a highway authority proposes to make an application under this section for an order relating to any highway (other than a classified road) they shall give at least two months notice of the proposal to: any district or parish council within the area affected or [in the case of Wales] to any Welsh council or community council within which the highway is situated*

Schedule 12 Highways Act 1980 (Part 1) contains the following additional provisions relating to applications under section 116, namely:

- a requirement to give formal notice (at least 28 days before the application is to be heard) specifying the time and place at which the application is to be made and the terms of the order applied for (by reference to an enclosed plan showing its effect): to the owners and occupiers of lands adjoining the highway; to any statutory undertakers having apparatus under, in, over, along or across the highway; to the Minister (in the case of a classified road); to any district or parish council, (or in the case of Wales) to any Welsh or community council;
- the requirement to display copies of the above notice at both ends of the highway to be stopped up or diverted;
- at least 28 days before the application is heard, the highway authority must have also published formal notice of its application in the *London Gazette* and in at least one newspaper circulating in the area in which the highway is situated and including within that notice a statement of a convenient place within the locality where a plan of the proposal may be inspected free of charge at all reasonable times.

Part II of Schedule 12 contains the following additional provisions relating to apparatus belonging to statutory undertakers, which is situated within a highway which has been stopped up under section 116:

- Statutory undertakers whose apparatus is under, in, upon, over, along or across the highway have the same powers and rights in respect of their apparatus as if the order authorising the highway to be stopped up or diverted had not been made.
- Where a highway has been stopped up or diverted under section 116, the statutory undertakers may (and shall if required to do so by the highway authority and at that council's expense): remove, replace or substitute their apparatus elsewhere.

The section 116 procedure for stopping up or diverting highways should only be used in the most straightforward and simplest of stopping ups when there is unlikely to be any campaign of opposition. Understandably, magistrates would be nervous about authorising the stopping up of any public road as being 'unnecessary' when there are other people who would insist that they use it on a daily basis. The requirement that any diverted route should be 'more commodious', suggests that under section 116 it is the convenience of the road user which is paramount, not the landowner.

The alternative statutory process for extinguishing highway rights is that contained in section 247 Town and Country Planning Act 1990 (and succeeding sections) for which different criteria apply. Under section 247 the Secretary of State may authorise the stopping up or diversion of any highway outside Greater London if he is satisfied that it is necessary to do so in order to enable development to be carried out in accordance with a planning permission granted under the Act or by a government department. The council of a London borough may also, for the same reasons, authorise the stopping up or diversion of a highway. Note also section 251 which states that where any land has been acquired or appropriated for planning purposes and is for the time being held by a local authority for the purposes which it was acquired or appropriated, the Secretary of State may by order extinguish any public right of way over the land if he is satisfied either that an alternative right of way has been or will be provided; or that the provision of an alternative right of way is not required.

Section 252 of the 1990 Act sets out the procedure for making highway extinguishment or diversion orders under that Act. Before making the order, the Secretary of State (or as the case may be the relevant London borough) must first publish in a local newspaper and in the *London Gazette* a notice: stating the general effect of the order; specifying a place where a copy of the draft order and of any relevant map or plan may be inspected by anyone free of charge at all reasonable hours, for a period of 28 days from publication of the notice and stating that any person may, within that period, give notice to the Secretary of State or London borough objecting to the making of the order. Not later than the date of publication of the notice the Secretary of State or London borough must also serve a copy of the notice (together with a copy of the draft order and of any relevant map or plan): on every local authority in whose area the highway is situated; on any national authority (where applicable); on any public utility having cables, mains, sewers, pipes or wires laid along, across, under, or over any highway to be stopped up or diverted. Copies of the notice must also be displayed in prominent positions at the end of so much of any highway as is proposed to be stopped up or diverted.

If during the 28-day objection period any objections are actually received by the Secretary of State or as the case may by the relevant London borough and is not withdrawn, the Secretary of State (where applicable) shall convene a public inquiry, save where in the special circumstances of the case (and in the absence of any objection from a local authority or public utility or transporter) it is considered that the holding of such an inquiry is unnecessary. Where it is a London borough which is making the order, the London borough shall notify the Mayor of London of any objections received and shall convene a public inquiry (save where there is no objection from any local authority, public utility or transporter and the Mayor of London decides in the special circumstances of the case that the holding of such an inquiry is unnecessary). What is important for the section 247 procedure is that there is already a planning permission in place to provide the justification for the extinguishment or diversion.

Whether a council opts for stopping up under section 116 of the Highways Act or section 247 of the Planning Act, what is important is that the need for any road or footpath closure is identified at the outset of a project so that the appropriate extinguishment procedures can be put in hand sooner rather than later and where possible concurrently with any compulsory purchase process to avoid duplication of work and project slippage. It may even be possible for any objections to a section 247 extinguishment to be heard at joint public inquiry with the compulsory purchase order.

7 Constitutional and procurement issues

As has already being seen, the first formal step in a housing regeneration project is to present an officer report to the appropriate council Cabinet or strategic committee seeking political 'in principle' support for the intended project. At that stage sufficient desktop research is likely to have been carried out to assess the feasibility of the proposed project, possible sources of funding and possible alternative options for delivering the project. All that officers are doing at this early stage is to introduce the idea of the project to their elected members and seek their members' permission to work the project up to the next stage, pending presentation of a further report. The following 'permissions' may be sought in that initial report and the resolutions which flow from it:

- permission to work up a detailed scheme to report back to the same Cabinet/committee for final sign off;
- permission to carry out a consultation exercise with those local residents who are affected and other known stakeholders;
- permission to appoint external consultants to evaluate and help work up viable scheme options;
- permission to apply for any grant funding which could assist in paying for the project;
- permission to initiate a procurement exercise to find a development partner (if required) or a contractor to build out the project (if the council chooses to go it alone). However, the final development partner/ building contractor appointment cannot be made until after a later Cabinet decision.
- for the elected members to authorise a limited budget to cover the initial costs outlined above.

80 Constitutional and procurement issues

On 8th December 2011 officers presented a report to Birmingham City Council's Cabinet committee property introducing the Meadway Regeneration Project and with the following stated purposes:

- *To inform Cabinet Committee Property of the work undertaken with the Homes and Communities Agency for the redevelopment of Meadway to provide new housing, retail and a shared service hub for public services.*
- *To seek approval for the Project Definition Document for the Meadway Regeneration Project and develop a preferred option to a Full Business Case, including options for delivery.*

That initial report also made the following recommendations, namely that Cabinet committee property:

- *Supported the work undertaken by the City Council with the Homes and Communities Agency and development of options for the regeneration project and that it approved the Project Definition Document as appended to the report;*
- *Approved the further development of a preferred option to Full Business Case;*
- *That Cabinet approved the allocation of £50,000, to be funded from the Public Sector Housing Advanced Design Fees Budget to progress the proposals to Full Business Case.*

On 16th March 2015 an officer report came back to Birmingham's Cabinet with a worked-up business case. The stated purposes of that second report were:

- *To inform Cabinet of an exciting opportunity to lead a major regeneration programme, working with the Homes and Communities Agency, to provide new mixed tenure housing, new retail premises and significant improvements to the public open space.*
- *To seek Cabinet approval to the Full Business Case for the first phase of the project and for the site assembly and procurement processes necessary to drive the project forward.*
- *To seek approval to accept £6.5M grant from the Homes and Communities Agency subject to the approval of funding conditions.*

Other recommendations in that Report which were necessary to progress the project included:

- *Authorising the Council's Director of Legal and Democratic Services to make a compulsory purchase order under Section 226 Town*

and Country Planning Act 1990 and Section 13 Local Government (Miscellaneous Provisions) Act 1976 in respect of the land and rights which are to be acquired;
- Authorising the Council's Director of Property to negotiate the acquisition of relevant interests and rights in land either voluntarily or through compulsory purchase if negotiations are not successful;
- Authorising the cessation of new lettings, the rehousing of existing tenants and the service of Initial and Final Demolition Notices under Schedule 5A Housing Act 1985;
- Authorising the appointment of contractors to undertake demolition;
- Approving the appropriation of public open space land held under the Open Spaces Act 1906 from General Fund to HRA (subject to the required statutory advertisement under Section 122 Local Government Act 1972 and with any objections being reported back to the Cabinet Member for Development Transport and the Economy);
- Authorising the marketing and disposal of defined land and with authority delegated to the Deputy Leader and Cabinet Member for Development Transport and the Economy, jointly with the Director of Property to accept the best bids for the phase one retail element, and to amend or vary the terms of the bid by up to 10%;
- To approve the procurement strategy to undertake the residential development for one or more housing developers using the Homes and Communities Agency Developer Partner Panel 2 Framework Agreement;
- To note that the contract award for the housing developer will be subject to approval by Cabinet in autumn 2016;
- Authorising the Head of Landscape Development to progress the retained open space to detailed design stage to support the Meadway redevelopment and to procure the open space works (subject funding availability) with a specialist landscape construction contractor through an approved tendering procedure;
- Authorising the Head of Transportation Services to develop highway proposals and progress the preferred option to detailed design.
- Authorising the appropriate statutory agreements under Sections 38 and 278 Highways Act 1980; as well as applications for highway stopping up orders under Section 247 Town and Country Planning Act; and appropriate Traffic Regulation Orders under Section 1 Road Traffic Regulation Act 1984;
- Giving the Director of Legal and Democratic Services general authority to take all necessary steps to give effect to the above recommendations.

On 26th July 2016 a third report was presented to Birmingham's Cabinet providing details of the procurement process which had been undertaken using the HCA Delivery Partner Panel Framework Agreement and making a recommendation as to how that contract should be awarded. The contract itself was stated to commence in August 2016 and run for three years.

Unless a council is intending to do everything itself (including the construction) there will be a need for an EU-compliant procurement process somewhere along the way. Depending on how the project is structured, the purpose of that procurement process will be to procure either a development partner to invest in the project or (if the council is going it alone) a building contractor. That appointed development partner or building contractor will then appoint its subcontractors. The council will also need to appoint its own professional team to oversee the project, including: lawyers; planning consultants; and an employer's agent.

Currently it is the Public Contracts Regulations 2015 which translate into domestic law EU Procurement Directives. The Regulations run to 131 pages and govern all public purchases (by local authorities) of goods, services and construction works above the following financial thresholds (as at 2017):

- £164,176 for supply services and design contracts;
- £4,104,394 for works contracts.

Note that these thresholds relate to the total cost of these contracts over their lifetimes, not to annual costs. There are also separate thresholds for purchases by central government, defence and security authorities; and public utilities. Therefore, if it is foreseeable that these thresholds may be exceeded, the correct EU procedures must be followed. Even where an intended contract is below the stated EU threshold, there will still need to be full compliance with the council's own contract standing orders, which will apply to council contracts of whatever value and may contain requirements additional to those imposed by statute. Contact standing orders can be found in the published constitution of every local authority.

Where EU procurement regulations apply, the starting point for any procurement will be the contract notice published in the *Official Journal of the European Union* (commonly shortened to the OJEU notice). The *Official Journal* is an electronic publication which circulates Europe-wide, alerting the market that a public sector contract is about to be placed and inviting expressions of interest. That contract notice will summarise what the contracting authority is wishing to purchase; the estimated value of the contract; the term of the contract (where applicable); the type of procurement procedure which the contracting authority intends to use; how prospective bidders can register their interests and the deadline for responding.

The 2015 Regulations allow contracting authorities a choice of procedures. The simplest is the open procedure. it is a one-stage procedure in which contractors bid against an invitation to tender (or ITT), with the contract being awarded to that which is most economically advantageous (over the life of the contract) from the point of view of the contracting authority. It is not just about the contracting authority accepting the lowest price; it can also take into account other factors such as: quality (including technical merit, aesthetic and functional characteristics, accessibility, design for all users, social, environmental and innovative characteristics and trading and its conditions); organisation, qualification and experience of staff assigned to perform the contract, where the quality of staff will have a significant impact on the performance of the contract; or after-sales service and technical assistance, delivery conditions (such as delivery date, delivery process and delivery period or a period of completion).

However, for major construction or partnership projects it is more likely that the contracting authority will opt for the two-stage 'restricted procedure': the first 'qualifying' stage of which is (through use of a scoring matrix) to weed out those prospective bidders whom, for whatever reason, are not considered sufficiently sound or capable to carry out the contract in the way the contracting authority would want. It is only those contractors who are shortlisted who are then invited to bid against the ITT. As with the open procedure, the contract will be awarded to that deemed most 'economically advantageous'. There are also, for the most complex projects, additional procedural options including: competitive dialogue and innovative partnerships.

Once the time for receipt of tenders has closed, there will be a process of evaluation with post-tender clarification questions, interviews and the scoring of each, before a recommendation can be made as to which of the bidders the contract should be awarded. Once that decision has been made, but before the contract can finally be signed off, there is a final process to be undertaken. Formal written notification will need to go out to each of the bidders advising them of the contract award, the contractor to whom it was awarded and the reasons why the contract was awarded in that way. There is then a 'stand-still' period, to provide anyone aggrieved by the outcome of the award an opportunity to raise challenges. There will also be publication of a contract award notice.

The purposes of these final procedures is to flush out any procurement challenges before the contract actually starts. Where a procurement challenge is made, the worst outcome for the contracting authority is the issue by the High Court of a 'decree of ineffectiveness', rendering void the contract award and the whole of the process leading up to it.

The problem with any major procurement is that it can become an expensive and time-consuming project in itself. It becomes a game played by each prospective bidder against the contracting authority and against every other bidder. The contracting authority has to ensure that it is sufficiently shielded against challenge. For each of the shortlisted bidders, submitting an EU-compliant bid involves massive investment on its part on the gamble that it may win the contract. That investment itself has to be priced into the bid, leading to higher costs overall for the contracting authority. It is for these reasons that many housing regeneration projects are procured through one of the several 'framework contracts' which are on the market.

Framework contracts occupy a special place in EU procurement law. They comprise a list of generic non-project-specific contract terms to which a selected panel of contractors have been appointed for a specific term (of up to four years) as a result of a competitive tender. The financial soundness and technical capabilities of each of those appointees will have been assessed and satisfied as part of that procurement process.

It is then open to any contracting authority to access that framework through an 'access agreement' and invite those panel members to bid for specific projects covered by that framework: known as 'call offs'. That framework contract will also incorporate transparent procedures which the contracting authority must follow to ensure equality of opportunity amongst panel members (sometimes referred to as a mini-tender) and which will ensure that the winning contractor is the one which is the most economically advantageous for the project in hand.

The Homes and Communities Agency's Development Partner Panel 3 (DPP3), launched on 31st July 2017, provides an example of a four-year framework agreement for the procurement of work to deliver residential-led development on public sector land. It replaces the earlier DPP2 which had become time-expired. The panel is intended to provide a simple and speedy Public Contract Regulations 2015 compliant procurement route for public sector organisations to appoint a developer or contractor. On its panel are 70 leading national and regional housing developers and contractors and it includes all activities necessary to construct housing and associated infrastructure, ranging from development and disposal of sites for residential use, to marketing and sales of homes. DPP3 is available free of charge to a wide range of local authorities, registered providers and other public sector bodies, including central government departments NHS trusts and educational establishments, to help them streamline their procurement process. By providing access to a pre-qualified list of housing developers, the panel is intended to make procurement more efficient by bringing significant time, cost and resource savings. The new panel is split into five regional lots (North East Yorkshire and The Humber; North West; Midlands; East and South East; South and South West) and aims to improve coverage and service, giving greater choice, flexibility and access to the market. The earlier

DPP1 and DPP2 panels have so far delivered over 43,500 homes, through 258 schemes over seven years.

In Chapter 9 we look in detail how a typical housing regeneration scheme might be documented. For the purposes of housing procurement it is also important that a set of draft indicative documentation is prepared and attached to the ITT against which prospective bidders can submit their tenders. Such draft documentation can only be indicative as the final version will need to be tailored to the successful bid. As part of the tender process it should be made clear to prospective bidders that requests for modifications to the model documentation will only be considered if that request forms part of the particular bid. When it comes to modifications to the indicative documentation, what is most important is that all prospective bidders are treated equally. Once a contract has been awarded, the opportunity to renegotiate unacceptable contract terms becomes much more limited without undermining the integrity of the entire procurement process. Once the contracting authority have formally accepted a tender, the parties are in a legally binding relationship, even if the development agreement itself is months away from being signed.

8 Funding considerations and options

What makes local authorities different from other registered housing providers is that councils pay stamp duty land tax (SDLT) on their land purchases. Stamp duty rates are progressive and can add an additional 12% on any single land purchase worth more than £1,500,000. That is assuming that the local authority does not also have to pay the 3% surcharge on the acquisition of second homes. For local authorities and any other non-exempt corporate bodies, the purchase of any dwelling is classed as a 'second home', putting those local authorities in the same tax bracket as any buy-to-let landlord.

For Treasury purposes, payment of stamp duty land tax by local authorities might be seen as a simple case of money passing from one public sector bank account to another. But the reality is that it potentially sucks money out of any regeneration budget. From the point of view of the local authority, it is dead money. Like VAT on petrol, it is also a tax-on-tax, in which SDLT is paid not only on the net purchase price but also on any VAT applicable to that purchase price. But SDLT is not the only tax which needs to be factored into the regeneration budget.

The other main property tax is value added tax (VAT), which applies to some property transactions but not others and in different ways. Dependent on the tax status of the particular piece of land which is being purchased, VAT can potentially add an additional 20% to the cost of land purchase (as well as the additional SDLT payable on that 20%). The issue with VAT is not so much whether the tax is triggered by the particular transaction but whether the paying party is VAT registered and therefore able to recover the VAT paid as an input. A third property tax is the community infrastructure levy, which is a local tax payable on the implementation of a planning permission. Although these are the main taxes, which are relevant to housing regeneration, the list is not exhaustive. Other tax issues include: capital gains tax, corporation tax, income tax, council tax, business rates and capital allowances amongst others. We now look in a little more detail at the main property taxes.

Stamp duty was one of the oldest property taxes, introduced in 1694 as a tax on documents. Payment of the tax was evidenced by a series of impressive red stamps embossed on the front of the document. The system remained almost unchanged until it was replaced in 2003 by Gordon Brown's new stamp duty land tax. In fact the only thing which the new tax has in common its predecessor is the name. The old one-page particulars delivered form was replaced by a stamp duty land tax return (SDLT1) the size of a self-assessment tax form and which is filed online. Calculating the tax is now so complicated that most practitioners use the online stamp duty land tax calculator. In short there are the following progressive tax bands fixed according to the purchase price:

- £0–£125,000   0%
- £125,000–£250,000   2%
- £250,000–£925,000   5%
- £925,000–£1,500,000 10%
- Above £1,500,000   12%

The above tax bands do not include the 3% surcharge for second homes or corporate purchases. There are also differences in the way residential and non-residential properties (including mixed use) are assessed. The general rule that SDLT is also paid on the VAT element of a transaction does not apply to a particular class of commercial transaction where the parties have agreed that it will be classed as the transfer of a business as a going concern (or TOGC). An example of a TOGC is an investment sale of an industrial estate where each of the units are rented out as a business. For the acquisition of a market rent commercial lease, SDLT will be paid on the capitalised value of the market rental. What is important for any housing regeneration project is the SDLT reliefs which are available. These can be found in official HMRC guidance, *Stamp Duty Land Tax: Relief for Land or Property Transactions* (published 6th May 2014). Those most applicable can be summarised as follows:

- **Multiple dwelling relief** (MDR), which applies where a single transaction comprises a number of dwelling houses and which enables SDLT to be calculated on the average price of each individual dwelling instead of the cumulative total price of all the dwellings. For simplicity, let us assume the purchase of ten dwelling houses each of which is valued at £500,000 – making a total of £5,000,000. Without MDR, SDLT would be assessed at the top 12% rate (plus the 3% surcharge). However, with MDR, SDLT is assessed at 5% (plus 3%) on the average £500,000 of each dwelling, multiplied by the number of dwellings.

88 *Funding considerations and options*

- **Compulsory purchase relief**, which applies if any property is acquired by a local authority under the umbrella of a compulsory purchase order but only if the acquiring authority's intention is to transfer the property on to another party for the purpose of redevelopment. Without that forward sale, normal SDLT would be payable on the acquisition. Compulsory purchase relief is not intended to make the transaction tax free. What it is intended to do is to avoid the double taxation which would otherwise apply on the council's acquisition of the property under the CPO, followed by the development partner's purchase of the same property from the acquiring authority. Compulsory purchase relief can still apply even to a voluntary sale to the acquiring authority under the backdrop of an unconfirmed CPO.
- **Planning obligation relief**, which applies where a developer acquires land from a third party on which to build a community facility (such as a school) which, on completion of construction, will be transferred to a local authority pursuant to a contractual commitment contained within a planning obligation made pursuant to section 106 Town and Country Planning Act 1990. Like compulsory purchase relief, the purpose of this exemption is to avoid double taxation on the developer's acquisition of the section 106 land from the third party – and again when the local authority takes an onward transfer of the completed school.
- **Transfer of property between companies** which are members of the same group when the transaction takes place.
- **Charity relief**, which applies when a charity buys land and property for charitable purposes.
- **Registered social landlord relief**, which applies where a registered social landlord (RSL) buys land and property where any of the following conditions are met:
    - most of the board members of the RSL are tenants living in properties from the RSL;
    - the seller of the property is a 'qualifying body', such as a local authority; or
    - a public subsidy funds the sale.

Look at any conveyancing document pre-1990 and it is unlikely that you will see any reference to VAT. That is because VAT had never applied to property transactions even though VAT had been introduced almost 20 years before to replace purchase tax. So, it was taken for granted that VAT would never apply. Land sales were classed within VAT legislation as 'exempt'. But all that changed at the beginning of the 1990s when the UK government became obliged by EU law to introduce a VAT regime for land transactions. What was originally intended to be 'light touch' has become a complicated tax structure which is applied piecemeal in the sense that the tax treatment is applied differently according to the particular class of property transaction, with some transactions being classed as 'exempt', others as zero rated, and a third category taxed at the full 20% rate. And as we have already seen, the imposition of 20% standard rate VAT on a land acquisition translates into an increase of at least 20% on the SDLT bill (unless the transaction can be classed as a TOGC). There is a further complication in that in some cases landowners can 'opt' to make their land VAT-taxable, even when it might otherwise be classed as 'exempt'. So why would you want to waive that tax exemption? Perhaps a result of detailed tax advice (see below). The default positions of different types of property transaction can be summarised as follows:

- Sales of residential accommodation are technically taxable but classed as 'zero rated' (which is why there is no VAT to pay on the purchase or rent of someone's home). 'Zero rating' has an advantage over 'exempt' when it comes to recovery of VAT paid out.
- A freehold sale of commercial new-build (within the first three years after construction) is compulsory rated at 20%;
- For other commercial transactions (including the grant of leases), whether or not VAT is charged on the rent or sale price depends upon whether the seller (or a previous owner) has notified HMRC of an 'option to tax'. Unless that option has been expressly exercised at some time in the past, the default position remains that the transaction is 'VAT exempt'.

VAT Notice 742: Land and Property (published 29th May 2012) sets out in detail the particular types of land transaction to which a liability for VAT will arise, whether as standard or through exercise of an option. For example, a lease or licence of garaging or parking spaces will normally be standard rated unless incidental to some other use.

If the rules for charging or not charging VAT on property transactions are complex, the rules for recovering paid VAT are even more so. The general rule is that an organisation that is registered for VAT and makes taxable supplies of goods and services can recover any VAT which it has had to pay out on its own purchases, as an input. Conversely an organisation which makes only exempt supplies, such as a housing association renting out homes, cannot recover its VAT. It is why it will rarely be viable for a housing association to purchase land on which there has been an option to tax. As local authorities provide a mixture of business, non-business and exempt supplies, the rules relating to the recovery of VAT are particularly complex. Official guidance is provided by *VAT Notice 749: Local Authorities and Similar Bodies*

90 *Funding considerations and options*

(updated 8th February 2016), which helps local authorities and other public bodies decide which activities are business or non-business. When commissioning major construction projects, local authorities must take particular care to ensure that any transactions related to that project are structured in a way which does not prejudice recovery of VAT on those construction costs.

Community infrastructure levy was introduced in the final years of the Blair/Brown government in their Planning Act 2008 and adopted by the incoming Coalition Government in its Community Infrastructure Levy Regulations 2010 as amended. It was introduced with the intention of replacing the financial contributions towards infrastructure improvements which would otherwise have had to be contained in section 106 planning obligations. It is a tariff-based system designed to cover the costs of all local infrastructure needs. It requires local planning authorities (known as 'charging authorities') to produce 'charging schedules' setting out their levy rates for different types of development. Here is a summary of how the CIL regime works:

- Under the 2010 Regulations a potential liability for CIL arises on a grant of planning permission for the construction of any new residential house or flat (of any size) or other development exceeding 100 square metres floor area (but not on residential extensions).
- A liability for CIL can only arise where the local planning authority has published a charging schedule within the Regulations. That charging schedule will apply different rates per square metre for different types of residential or commercial development. The money raised through a charging schedule must have a direct link to the expenditure required to pay for infrastructure improvements falling on the public purse and which are required to accommodate new developments. An example of one of the first charging schedules is that published by the Mayor for London in April 2012 and which was intended to raise funding for the Crossrail Project, running east–west across London between Shenfield and Maidenhead and which charges between £20 and £50 per metre of new development, depending on the particular London borough within which the proposed development will take place. The schedule also provides nil bands for development related to the provision of health services, education, charitable purposes and social housing. As at February 2016 the Mayor's schedule had already raised £280,000,000 for Crossrail, significantly less than the £600,000,000 which has been hoped for during the life of this particular schedule (which is due to be replaced December 2017). CIL payable under the Mayor's schedule is in addition to any other CIL which the developer may be required to pay under any other charging schedule published by the particular London borough within which the development will take place.

Funding considerations and options 91

- On the grant of a new planning permission, the charging authority (which is the local planning authority) will issue a liability notice in respect of the CIL which will be due in respect of that particular development. However, the obligation to pay that CIL will not actually arise until development is formally commenced. Developers are under a legal obligation to notify the charging authority when development is about to start and provide details of the person who has accepted responsibility for payment of the CIL. If that preliminary notice is not given to the charging authority, the obligation to pay CIL will have been triggered by the start of development itself, in which case the charging authority will make its own assessment of who is responsible for payment in accordance with the default provisions set out in the regulations. Once issued, a liability notice is registered as a local land charge, which will be removed from the register on payment of the CIL.
- The 2010 Regulations exempt charities from any requirement to pay CIL for developments on their own land which will be used for charitable purposes. There is also a social housing relief, which applies to developments by registered providers and local authorities and which is calculated according to complex formulae.

Like SDLT, a local authority's payment of CIL on a development project is a case of money being taken out of one public purse and being transferred to another. Only more so, because in many cases it will be the same local authority which is paying the CIL as is receiving it, but in different budgets. But again, it sucks money out of the regeneration pot. For any regeneration project, it is therefore important at the outset:

- to identify what property taxes are likely to be involved and to budget for them; and
- to structure the transaction (or multiple transactions) in the way which is considered most tax efficient. For the largest projects this will inevitably involve commissioning external tax advice from an accountancy firm on exactly how the transactions should best be structured.

In the second part of this chapter, we look at the several ways in which a housing regeneration project can be funded. Options include:

- cross-subsidisation through the building of homes for outright sale on the open market;
- prudential borrowing;
- private finance arranged through a development partner;
- the availability of grants.

92 *Funding considerations and options*

In many cases the costs of funding a housing regeneration is likely to comprise a mix of various funding mechanisms. We look in more detail at each of these funding mechanisms.

As we have already seen, by using its powers under the Local Authorities (Land) Act 1963 it is theoretically possible for a local authority to build homes on its own land and sell them on the open market. But there are clear disadvantages in it attempting to go it alone, whether directly or through its own subsidiary company. Building houses for market sale is not a local authority's core business.

House building is a specialised industry. Housebuilders have to be registered with the National House Building Council or something similar, to be able to offer the NHBC or comparable warranties which mortgage lenders require before they will advance money on the purchase of a new property. And they have to know the market. Registered housebuilders also can access external finance, which local authorities would be unable to access directly. For this reason, where a public sector regeneration project includes the development of housing for outright sale it will be usual for the local authority to transfer across its vacant land to the development partner as soon as the last tenant or leaseholder has vacated. Whether that land transfer is at market value or at a nominal £1 consideration is a matter for negotiation in each individual case, driven in part by what is most financially efficient for the scheme.

In a typical regeneration project, the development partner will take over the vacated buildings, demolish them and then build out the new development. The new dwellings will then be offered for sale by the developer on the open market. The success of this approach to cross-subsidy is of course dependent on construction costs being kept within budget and a healthy property market at the point of sale. The terms negotiated between the council and its development partner may also allow the council to share in any excess profits if the prices at which the new homes can eventually be sold exceed expectations.

The principle behind prudential borrowing is to enable local authorities to access the finance they need to invest to save. Part I Chapter 1 of the Local Government Act 2003 provides (under the heading 'Capital Finance Etc') the statutory framework for prudential borrowing. Section 1 of that Act states (under the heading 'Power to Borrow'):

A local authority may borrow money –

(a) For any purpose relevant to its functions under any enactment, or
(b) For the purposes of the prudent management of its financial affairs.

Under the heading 'Control of Borrowing' section 2 states:

(1) A local authority may not borrow money if doing so would result in a breach of –

    (a) the limit for the time being determined by or for it under Section 3, or
    (b) any limit for the time being applicable to it under Section 4.

(2) The Secretary of State may in relation to specific borrowing by a particular local authority by direction disapply Subsection 1(b) so far as relating to any limit for the time being applicable under Section 4(1).

(3) A local authority may not without the consent of the Treasury borrow otherwise than in sterling.

(4) This Section of applies to borrowing under any power for the time being available to a local authority under any enactment, whenever passed.

Section 3 requires each local authority to determine and keep under review how much money it can afford to borrow. In the case of the Greater London Authority (or for any derivative body such as Transport for London) it is the London Mayor who will determine (in consultation with the London Assembly or derivative body) and keep under review how much that organisation can afford to borrow. The Secretary of State has made regulations about the performance of this duty and the factors which must be taken into account when making those determinations.

Section 4 gives the Secretary of State general power to make regulations, for national economic reasons, setting limits in relation to the borrowing of money by local authorities. The Secretary of State may also by specific direction set limits in relation to the borrowing of money by a particular local authority to ensure that the authority does not borrow more than it can afford. Those limits are currently set out in the Local Authorities (Capital Finance and Accounting) (England) Regulations 2003. In assessing their affordable borrowing limits and in the application of prudential borrowing, local authorities are also required to comply with CIFA's Prudential Code for Capital Finance in Local Authorities.

In his 27th June 2016 House of Commons briefing paper *Local Government in England: Capital Finance*, author Mark Sandiford explains how the local authority capital finance regime works in practice and provides specific examples of prudential borrowing and the options which are currently available to local authorities. He explains that local authorities may borrow money from different sources, including borrowing on the markets, using

94 *Funding considerations and options*

the Public Works Loan Board (PWLB) and by the issue of municipal bonds. However what councils cannot do directly is to mortgage their property.

The PWLB has a history stretching back to 1793 when it was set up as a non-ministerial government department. Since July 2002 it has been managed as part of the UK Debt Management Office. Even today it remains the biggest lender to local government because of its below market interest rates. Until October 2010 it offered an interest rate between 0.15% and 0.20% above the government's own borrowing costs – since raised to 1%. Some larger local authorities then began to investigate whether they could get a better interest rate from a bond issue. However, in its 2012 Budget the government introduced a new 'certainty rate', discounting from 1% to 0.8% and available from 1st November 2012. A further discount to 0.6% for borrowing regarding an infrastructure project nominated by a local enterprise partnership was introduced in November 2013.

Local authorities have always had the power to issue bonds, allowing them to raise substantial capital immediately, to be repaid at a specified point in the future. Sandiford says it would be possible for a local authority to issue bonds as part of a TIF (tax increment financing) scheme, which enables them to borrow money for infrastructure projects against the anticipated increase in tax receipts resulting from that infrastructure. TIF schemes in England have so far been based on business rate revenues, as being the only local authority tax revenues which are likely to be directly affected by infrastructure projects. Where bonds are issued as part of a TIF process, money would be obtained up front by selling the bonds and then be paid back from the additional tax revenues resulting from the public investment. It is a scheme which is popular in the United States. But a local authority will have serious financial problems if the anticipated tax revenues do not materialise and the local authority is unable to repay the bonds, to which Sandiford points to the 2013 bankruptcy of Detroit City Council. However, Sandiford also points to the example of Warrington Council's August 2015 £150 million bond issue to fund the redevelopment of Warrington town centre, and which has a 40-year repayment period. Warrington will seek to repay the bonds from the proceeds of this redevelopment, from future business rates revenue or from future property sales and rental.

A new corporate entity, known as the UK Municipal Bonds Agency, was established in 2016 by 56 shareholding local authorities and the Local Government Association. Its purpose is to facilitate the issuing of bonds by smaller local authorities and to obtain a competitive price for their bonds within the conventional bond market. In particular it is intended that the agency will offer a lower rate of interest than the PWLB, which would be achieved by obtaining a good credit rating for the agency based on the credit ratings of participating councils. The Agency is open to both shareholder authorities and councils elsewhere. Councils wishing to participate in a bonds issue will have to supply sufficient financial information for bond-buyers to be able to judge the Agency's collective creditworthiness. The services of the Agency will be financed by a levy upon any bonds issued, of ten basis points for members and 15 basis points for non-members.

As we have already seen, local authorities with retained housing stock became self-financing from April 2012, meaning that they may borrow the against rental income to finance investment in their existing stock and new housebuilding up to a centrally set limit and which is recorded in a separate ring-fenced HRA account. There is a total national cap on HRA borrowing, which was initially set at £29.8 billion, which is less than would apply if the Prudential Code was applied to councils' borrowing against their HRAs. However, as part of its December 2013 Autumn Statement, the Chancellor increased local authority HRA borrowing limits by £150 million in 2015–2016 and a further £150 million in 2016–2017, allocated on a competitive basis and from the sale of vacant high value social housing. That funding was intended to support around 10,000 new affordable homes to form part of the Local Growth Fund, available to local authorities who have a proposal agreed by their local enterprise partnership and with expectation of partnership working with housing associations or through joint ventures. Sandiford also mentions the number of legal authorities which have established their own companies to build additional housing in their areas and which, through their companies, have greater flexibility with regard to taking finance and the choices around building.

Finally, Sandiford reminds us of the private finance initiative, as a finance model launched in 1992, under which a private sector partner would typically design, build, finance and operate public facilities under a long-term contract of up to 30 years. During the contract period, the commissioning local authority would pay the contractor for its use of the facility. It was once a popular option for financing major projects. However, in recent years, and particularly since the financial crisis, the number of new PFI projects has fallen sharply. In 2014–2015 just seven projects were agreed, with only a few more in the pipeline in March 2015.

In December 2012 the Treasury published *A New Approach to Public Private Partnership*, which sought to address the issues with the existing PFI regime and which proposed a new 'PF2' to replace it. According to *Construction News* (23rd March 2017), only six projects have so far been signed off under PF2, namely: the Midland Metropolitan Hospital at Smethwick and five batches of schools procured by the Education Funding Agency under the Priority Schools Programme.

The National Housing Federation has identified the following sources of grant funding for housing regeneration:

- **The Affordable Homes Programme 2015–2018 (AHP)** – which was launched to provide £1.7 billion of capital funding to deliver a range of a new affordable homes. Allocations of just over £1 billion will deliver around 58,000 homes outside London.
- **The shared ownership and affordable homes programme 2016** – was launched at the Autumn Statement to provide £4.7 billion capital funding (comprising a mix of new funding and unallocated AHP) to deliver 153,000 new affordable homes for shared ownership and rent to buy as well as specialist and supported housing.
- **The Mayor's Housing Covenant 2015–2018 (MHC)** – which provides £1.25 billion of investment to deliver 42,000 affordable homes.
- **The Homes for Londoners: Affordable Homes Programme 2016–2021 (HfL)** – which provides over £3 billion capital funding to build at least 90,000 homes in London by 2021 (and again which is a mix of new funding and unallocated MHC) and which will be used to provide homes for London affordable rent; London living rent and London shared ownership.
- **The Homebuilding Fund** – (which is aimed at small builders, community builders, custom builders, and regeneration specialists) and which provides £3 billion loan finance (at commercial rates) to cover the development costs of building homes for sale or rent, and the cost of site preparation and infrastructure needed to enable housing development and to prepare land for housing.
- **The Estate Regeneration Fund** – which provides £140 million of recoverable investments aimed at accelerating and improving estate regeneration and which is available for five years from 2016 to 2021.

The list is not of course exhaustive and new initiatives will be launched as existing schemes are closed.

This chapter would not be complete without the obligatory warning about state aid and the need for due diligence to ensure that any funding arrangement between the council and its development partner does not infringe European rules intended to ensure fair competition. The Department for Business Innovation and Skills explains the subject in its July 2015 document, *State Aid: the Basics*.

State aid can occur when public resources are used to provide assistance to another organisation in a way which gives it an unfair advantage over other organisations. It can distort competition in a way which harms consumers

Funding considerations and options 97

and other companies in the EU who are competing for the same business. State Aid will arise where the following four conditions are satisfied:

- Some form of assistance has been provided by a public body or using public resources.
- That assistance gives an advantage to one or more undertakings over others. For this purpose, an 'undertaking' is an organisation engaged in economic activity involving putting goods or services on the market. And an 'advantage' can take many forms including a grant, loan, tax break or use of a public asset free of charge or at less than market price. Essentially it is something which the undertaking could not get in the normal course of business.
- That assistance distorts or has the potential to distort competition by strengthening the recipient by comparison to its competitors.
- The assistance affects trade between member states (for which it is enough to show that the particular product or service is tradeable between member states, even if the recipient does not itself export to other EU markets).

Where it is considered possible that state aid may apply, any of the following solutions are suggested:

- Redesigning the arrangement in a way which clearly does not infringe state aid rules.
- By using one of the approved mechanisms set up to allow state aid in particular circumstances, as detailed in the *State Aid Manual*. For example, state aid can legally be granted in the event of genuine market failure, to the extent that it is necessary, justified and compatible with EU rules. In general, the European Commission will base approvals on whether aid is:
  (a) in terms of proportionality, the minimum necessary to remedy the failure;
  (b) whether it will really incentivise the organisation receiving it to change its behaviour;
  (c) whether it is an appropriate way to address the failure;
  (d) that as a matter of balance the aid is appropriate.
- Addressing the state aid question sooner rather than later, so as to minimise project delays. In particular, it is recommended that a project is checked for state aid before any money is paid out. This will avoid the worst-case scenario where money has to be clawed back because it infringes state aid rules and with the expensive contractual issues which would flow from that eventuality.

98 *Funding considerations and options*

- Using the General Block Exemption Regulation (GBER), which provides a simple way to assist measures considered not to unduly distort competition. Use of GBER does not require prior approval, but the Commission must be notified within 20 working days using the SANI online system. Examples of activities for which assistance can be provided under GBER include: environmental protection; research, development and innovation; recruitment and employment aid for disadvantaged workers or those with disabilities; making good damage caused by natural disasters; social aid for transport for residents in remote regions; broadband infrastructure; culture and heritage conservation; and sport.

The official guidance urges policymakers to understand and manage the risks which state aid might pose to their projects. The impact of any unnotified measure being later found by the Commission to be incompatible will involve removal of the scheme and possible recovery of aid already given. More detail about state aid can be found in the 102-page *State Aid Manual* published by the Department for Business Innovation and Skills in July 2015. Specialist state aid teams can also advise on process and comment on documents. There is on the BIS State Aid website a self-assessment form to help structure the information the teams will need in order to provide advice. However, tailored advice can usually only be given to public bodies. Other organisations must obtain their advice independently. In the case of a major housing regeneration project, a risk of state aid is most likely to arise where a local authority lends money to its private sector development partner below market rate. The temptation for doing this may be that the local authority is able to prudentially borrow at a cheaper rate than its development partner can borrow on the open market, leading to a cheaper project overall.

9 Documenting the project

From the moment a contracting authority formally notifies a bidder that their tender has been accepted, the parties are in a binding contractual relationship. This is in spite of the fact that the development agreement itself may be still many months away from being signed. This contractual relationship derives from the traditional common law principles of offer, acceptance and consideration as being the core ingredients of any contract.

The 'offer' in this case is the submitted tender. The 'acceptance' is the contracting authority's formal written and unconditional notification to the successful bidder that their tender has been accepted. The 'invitation to tender' (or ITT), issued as part of the statutory procurement process, is not technically an offer at all. It is a 'call for offers'. Like an auction brochure, the ITT will describe the contract which the contracting authority wishes to enter into and the terms and conditions on which it is willing to contract. Whilst the core purpose of an ITT is to comply with statutory procurement procedures, the ITT should also be regarded as a sales document. This means that it has to be contractor-friendly. An ITT which is too onerous or one sided, may not only deter prospective bidders, it may also lead to higher bids as commercial developers try to price in those additional risks or obligations. Accompanying the ITT will be a 'tender pack', which is a formidable bundle of documents comprising everything a prospective bidder needs to formulate an informed bid. The tender pack will contain full information about the land to be redeveloped and its title. It is also good practice to include, within the tender pack, indicative drafts of all documentation which the successful bidder will be expected to sign. That documentation can of course only be indicative because it will need to be tailored to the terms of the successful bid. Without full indicative documentation against which prospective bidders can make their bids, all that will be left is an 'agreement to agree', which can never be enforced in law.

The 'consideration' given by each party to the other in this common law scenario is their commitment to enter into a development agreement (and to comply with the terms of that agreement as if it had already been entered into). The existence of that common law contractual relationship means that, once a tender has been put forward and formally accepted, neither party can unilaterally withdraw from that contractual relationship without legal consequences. There is good reason for this. The successful bidder will have already invested significant resources in making the bid in the expectation that (if accepted) they will be commissioned to carry out the work. The contracting authority will have invested time and resources in undertaking a statutory procurement process, as a result of which other competing bids would have already been rejected. But the consequences to a contracting authority of a failed contract may not just be the time and cost of undertaking another procurement process. With many housing regeneration projects, time is money: particularly where the project is partially grant funded. Like a mortgage offer, most offers of grant funding are time limited. Much grant funding has to be fought for in competition with other worthy projects. There is never enough money for everyone. It follows that if there are any delays in getting a grant-funded project under way, that grant funding might be diverted to a different worthy cause.

Notwithstanding that a contractual relationship – of sorts – already exists from the point of 'acceptance', there is still an uncomfortable transition between that point and the date the development agreement is actually signed. As will be seen, it will be the development agreement which will become the framework document for the project and the first point of reference as regards any issue between the parties as regards taking forward the regeneration. Until the point the development agreement is actually signed, what constitutes the 'contract' is what is contained within the successful bid. And as that bid would have been made against the ITT (and everything else contained within the tender pack), as well as any other pre-tender communications or clarifications passing between the contracting authority and the pool of prospective bidders, those additional documents and communications will also form part of that contract. So, if the parties are already in a contractual relationship, why is it necessary to sign a development agreement at all?

It is all about tidiness. It is about putting everything in one place. It is about creating a central point of reference. It is about certainty. And there is also the legal question of enforceability. Whilst offer, acceptance and consideration may suffice to create a binding contract at common law, for contracts involving the sale, leasing or mortgaging of real estate there is an additional legal requirement: section 2 of the Law of Property (Miscellaneous Provisions) Act 1989. The basic requirements of section 2 are:

- the document must be in writing;
- the document must contain *all* the terms of the transaction;

Documenting the project 101

- the transactional terms must be comprised either within a single document, which is signed by all parties to the transaction, or in separate identical parts which are 'exchanged' at the point the contract becomes binding.

Without strict compliance with section 2, the contract is unenforceable. And as most development agreements involve, at some stage of the process, the transfer or leasing of land, the agreement must be compliant with section 2. The case of *Jelson Ltd v Derby City Council* [2000] JPL 203 is a reminder of what can happen when it does not comply. The *Jelson* case did not involve the enforceability of a development agreement but a section 106 planning obligation which required the developer, amongst other things, to transfer part of the development, comprising affordable housing, to a registered housing association. However, when the developer, later and for its own reasons, declined to comply with its obligation to transfer land in the way the agreement required, Derby Council issued legal proceedings to force Jelson to comply. But the proceedings failed because Deputy Judge Mackie QC ruled that the section 106 obligation was unenforceable because no named housing association had been made party to the agreement. In fact, at the point the section 106 agreement was entered into, no specific housing association had even been identified to take the transfer. Therefore, it could not be said that all parties to the transaction had signed the contract for the purposes of section 2 of the 1989 Act. Consequentially, there was no land transaction which could be enforced. What was notable about the *Jelson* case was how quickly its lessons were forgotten. Post-*Jelson*, many section 106 planning obligations continued to be structured in the same way with obligations on the part of developers to convey properties to – yet to be identified – housing association transferees. It was then fortuitous that, ten years later, and in another section 106 planning obligation case, a different judge took a more pragmatic view as to how section 2 of the 1989 Act should be applied in planning obligation cases, when he said:

> *it seems to me that it would substantially frustrate the statutory scheme contained in Section 106 of the 1990 Act to interpret Section 2 of the 1989 Act as invalidating section 106 agreements which benefit third parties such as Milebush. I can't believe that that can have been the legislative intention.*

The case of *Milebush Properties Ltd v Tameside MBC and Hillingdon LBC* [2010] EWHC 1022 (Ch), which was heard before Arnold J, concerned a developer's section 106 obligation to make up a service road and grant rights of way over it to neighbouring owners, who were not party to that

102 *Documenting the project*

agreement. However, before the rights of way could be granted, Tameside Council purchased the completed development as an investment. The issues then was whether Tameside, as the successor in title, could be forced to grant a right away in the terms which neighbouring owner, Milebush, wanted. Tameside offered Milebush a right of away on terms which were more restrictive than those to which Milebush considered that they were entitled. The company sought a judicial declaration to that effect. Tameside pleaded that the obligation to grant a right of way was of no effect because Milebush had not been party to the original section 106 agreement as required by section 2 of the 1989 Act. But this time the argument failed. The *Milebush* case went to appeal ([2011] EWCA Civ 270) but not on a 1989 Act issue. The only issue for the appeal was whether it was appropriate for the court to grant a private declaration in the context of a statutory agreement, which was generally governed by public law principles. Appeal judges ruled that Milebush were entitled to their declarations. Section 2 of the 1989 Act has yet to be tested in the context of a development agreement (which is more in the nature of a private contract than a section 106 planning obligation). But there is no reason to think that section 2 would be any less strictly applied.

Even if there are issues of enforceability before a development agreement is signed, what will hold the transaction together is the goodwill of the parties. There is mutuality of interest. The contracting authority want to deliver the project (otherwise they would not have put it out to tender). The developer wants the contract (otherwise they would not have put in their bid). Both parties have invested heavily in bringing matters to that stage. Any contractual disputes will come later after the documentation has been signed.

Statutory procurement procedures do not permit wholesale renegotiation of a contract which has already been awarded. That would be unfair on other bidders. However, there is a need to tailor the indicative documents contained within the tender pack into something which incorporates the detailed terms of the successful bid and is otherwise fit for purpose. That process may itself involve tortuous rounds of negotiation to achieve something which is workable and sufficiently reflects the intentions of the parties. We now look in more detail at the structure of a typical development agreement.

The development agreement is the key reference point for any regeneration project. It is a working document, regulating the legal relationship between the parties throughout the life of the project. It is intended to incorporate and put into one place everything which the parties have agreed in the process leading up to acceptance of the successful tender – and since. As such, one need normally refer back no earlier than the date of the development agreement to ascertain what the parties have agreed. For

Documenting the project 103

that reason, the development agreement will generally be the first formal document which the parties will enter into, post-tender, to record that legal relationship. That is because the development agreement is also a framework document.

Standing behind the development agreement will be many other future documents which the parties will need to enter into to fully document the project. Depending on the circumstances of the case, these other documents are likely to include:

- appointments of professional team and subcontractors;
- collateral warranties from the above;
- CPO indemnity agreement (if the local authority is going to be using its compulsory purchase to assemble the development site for transfer on to the development partner);
- a lease or freehold transfer of the development site from the council to the development partner (or registered provider in the case of land earmarked for affordable housing), such transfer or lease to take place either once the redevelopment has been completed or earlier if agreed;
- a nominations agreement, if the local housing authority is to have the right to nominate future occupants of the affordable housing from its housing waiting list.

The list is not exhaustive. A well-drawn development agreement will also contain indicative drafts of each of these subsidiary documents. This is not to say that there will be no negotiated variations to meet changing circumstances. But the drafts provide the reference point. Before looking in more detail at the rights and obligations of each party, we first need to remind ourselves as to what each party brings to the regeneration table.

For the contracting authority, it is its ability to use its statutory powers to assemble the development site and overcome third-party rights and interests which might otherwise derail the project; to access grant funding as well as being (in most cases) the major landowner.

For the development partner, it is the expertise and resources it can call upon to design and build out a major project as well as its ability to access external sources of funding for the project. If the development partner is a joint venture vehicle or special purposes vehicle, the contracting authority may also insist that a 'parent company guarantee' is given, which means that if at any stage the development partner becomes insolvent or otherwise cannot fulfil its contractual commitments, there is a more substantial party against which the contracting authority can seek legal recourse. The development agreement will also need to cover the three stages of any design and build development project, which are: pre-construction; the construction stage; and the final post-construction stage.

No building work can start without a vacant site; without planning permission; without ground surveys and until any third-party rights and interests which might otherwise interfere with development have been neutralised. And there is also the need to ensure that the development can be fully funded and will be economically viable for both parties. These will be crystallized in a set of preconditions (or conditions precedent) which have to be satisfied before any construction can actually start. The most important precondition is the need for a satisfactory planning permission. A planning permission is satisfactory if it is granted free from any onerous condition. A planning condition is 'onerous' if it threatens to undermine the future financial viability of the development. An example might be a planning condition prohibiting the sale of alcohol in a restaurant or restricting its opening hours. It would normally be for the developer to state in the development agreement what type of planning conditions it would regard as onerous.

For a typical regeneration project, it would be for the development partner to design the scheme for the council's approval (as landowner). Once such landowner approval has been obtained, the next stage is for the development partner to make the planning application. In many cases it will be the same local authority which commissioned the project which now has to decide whether (and if so on what terms) planning permission should be granted. This then begs the question as to what should happen if planning permission is either refused or granted on onerous terms. If it is the development partner which made the planning application, then (subject to the terms of the development agreement) it is the developer which will have a statutory right of appeal to the Secretary of State. Council planning officers are then in the difficult position of having to defend a planning refusal against a scheme which other council officers have put forward. It is why every development agreement will contain a clause stating that nothing in it is intended to fetter or in any way prejudice any regulatory decision which the local authority may have to make in exercise of any statutory discretion.

If planning permission cannot be obtained on terms which are sufficiently satisfactory to enable construction to commence, or if there is a failure of other preconditions, the project may collapse at that point if the situation cannot be remedied within the contractual timescale. But that collapse will not be without legal consequences. The development partner may have already incurred substantial costs in designing the scheme, carrying out surveys and pursuing a planning application (perhaps even to the point of appeal). It will want reimbursement (or at least a substantial contribution) from the local authority landowner towards those abortive costs. It is why a well-drawn development agreement should also contain detailed provisions setting out where the financial liabilities will fall should the project collapse at that early stage. But suppose a satisfactory planning permission is granted and all other preconditions are satisfied. Construction can then commence. At that point the contract (having become unconditional) moves into its construction stage.

As well as the development partner itself, there will also be specialist teams of subcontractors dealing with every part of the construction, including: quantity surveyors; lift engineers; mechanical and electrical engineers and many others. Whilst those subcontractors are not directly party to the development agreement, they will each contract separately and directly with the commissioning landowner via collateral warranties, through which they warrant their individual skills and workmanship. Those warranties may also be assignable to tenants, purchasers or funders of the completed development. The existence of a collateral warranty means that if the construction is later found to be defective, the party in whose favour the collateral warranty is given will have direct legal recourse against the contractor whose work is at fault. The guarantee provided by a collateral warranty can subsist for up to 12 years from completion of construction, but may be expressed to be for a lesser period. Of course, that guarantee is only as strong as the contractor providing that warranty, unless backed by insurance. Perhaps the most well-known collateral warranty is the NHBC certificate issued by the National House Building Council to the buyers of new houses and flats, which guarantees the property against structural problems for up to ten years, or for two years in respect of anything else.

The development agreement will set out a timetable for completion of construction, with target dates (which may be extended if circumstances dictate) and with longstop dates, beyond which there may be serious legal consequences. There may be contractual provisions requiring payment of liquidated damages by the development partner to the contracting authority. Liquidated damages can be seen as an attempt to pre-estimate the financial losses which an innocent contracting party would be likely to suffer as a result of delays in completing construction. This might include a delayed income stream from the completed development. A major development contract is also likely to contain change-control mechanisms, enabling either party to propose changes to a development specification for the approval of the other party, at any point during the construction process. Any agreed changes to the development specification are also likely to mean corresponding changes in the final contract price. The development agreement will provide the development partner and its contractors with access to the vacant development side to demolish existing buildings and carry out the redevelopment, and setting out the terms and conditions of that access. At that stage of development, it is likely that the commissioning authority will still own the land subject to the developer's rights under the agreement. Any transfer of title will come after the redevelopment has been completed. It follows that the final stage of a redevelopment is the point at which construction has reached a 'practical completion', which is the point at which the development is substantially complete, subject to rectification of minor defects (to be set out in a snagging list). It is at the point of practical completion (or shortly thereafter) that any transfers or leasing of the completed development will take place. One of the extraneous factors affecting the financial viability of a completed development is the buoyancy of the housing market at the point of completion, particularly in the common situation where the cost of social housing provision is cross-subsidised by the construction of other housing for outright sale. It is generally the development partner which will take the financial risk of a poor housing market for the outright sale properties. But suppose the buoyancy of the housing market exceeds expectations. Is it then the development partner which will be entitled to all of the excess profits? It is precisely to cater for that eventuality that most development agreements will contain overage provisions by which excess profits from the scheme will be divided between the contracting authority and its development partner according to agreed formulae.

Where a development scheme involves the contracting authority making a compulsory purchase order, it is likely that it will want a development partner which is financing the project to enter into a CPO indemnity agreement (IA). Under the IA, the council will exercise its CPO powers on behalf of and at the expense of its development partner. It is then that development partner which will reimburse to the local authority its costs in acquiring individual properties under the CPO in addition to the council's legal and administrative costs in making and implementing the CPO.

Larger redevelopment schemes are commonly tripartite, meaning that as well as the local authority and its development partner, there is also on board a registered housing provider. Many development agreements include provision for the local authority to enter into a freehold transfer of the new-build affordable housing directly to the registered provider at nil consideration. That registered provider rule will then manage the affordable housing according to its own policies, but usually subject to the right of the local authority transferor to nominate (through a separate nominations agreement) from its own housing waiting list, the occupants of those new dwellings. For former local authority 'secure' tenants, who were displaced as part of the scheme regeneration, there may also be an obligation on the registered provider for something which – contractually at least and as near as possible – offers the similar security and associated rights (including the right to buy at discount) as were previously available to those tenants under their HRA tenancies. In some cases, the arrangement is structured in a way which enables the local authority to take a lease-back from the register provider of those new-build properties being used to re-house local authority tenants who have been displaced. As those former secure tenants will now again be renting directly from the local authority (under that lease-back arrangement) their statutory security and right-to-buy will continue as before.

In a regeneration scheme the phrase 'development partner' is used for a reason. Whilst the regulatory process of procuring a development partner has to be arm's length, once the contractual arrangements are in place, it is essential for the success of a regeneration project that the parties are able to work together in the spirit of partnership. The development agreement and its associated documentation should then provide only a backdrop to what becomes a living working relationship involving regular meetings and day-to-day today contact between the parties to review progress, address obstacles, and generally steer the project through to a satisfactory completion. Any registered provider which is an integral part of that scheme of regeneration will also be represented in many partnership meetings.

The term 'partnering' in the context of building construction was coined to describe a new type of contractual relationship where the commissioning client and its contractor (and subcontractors) and everyone else in the supply chain works together in the spirit of trust and with a view to achieving an outcome which is 'win–win'. This new approach became popular following Sir Michael Latham's 1994 Report *Contracting the Team* in which he criticised the adversarial approach of a traditional building contract.

Partnering describes a collaborative approach which encourages openness and trust between the contracting parties. They have to become dependent on each other for the success of the project. It demands a change in culture, attitudes and procedures throughout the supply chain. From time to time a project board (comprising commissioning authority, development partner, and registered provider) will encounter a new issue, unexpected event or opportunity which cannot be addressed within the terms of the existing development agreement. It may then be necessary to quickly negotiate and document a Variation Agreement to accommodate the changed circumstances.

10 Local authority companies

As we have already seen, there are some examples of existing housing regeneration projects which involve a local authority working through its own council-controlled company (in which it is the only shareholder). However, there are many more examples of local authorities working in partnership with their development partners through the vehicle of a joint venture company, on which it is represented.

When things are going well most legal authority companies purr quietly in the background. It is only when things go to disastrously wrong that they hit the headlines. The most notable example of such a disaster was the 1994 case of *Credit Suisse v Allerdale Borough Council* ([1995] 1 Lloyd's Rep 215). It involved not a housing regeneration project but instead a joint venture to redevelop the old Keswick railway station site to create a leisure complex to include swimming pool, conference centre, squash and tennis courts. The cost of providing those facilities would then be cross-subsidised by the simultaneous development and sale of timeshare accommodation. But an initial £6 million would first have to be raised to kick start the development.

The council could not have provided this money directly without going outside its statutory spending and borrowing constraints. Instead, the council set up its own limited company 'Allerdale Development Company' and guaranteed its borrowings. On that basis Credit Suisse agreed to fund the development. Before entering into the arrangement, Allerdale took senior counsel's advice and wrote to the district auditor setting out its proposal. A financial projection showed that profits from timeshare sales would pay for the leisure complex with cash to spare. No one foresaw the 1988–1989 property market collapse. Only 175 timeshare weeks were sold out of 1,000. The company could not repay the first instalment on its loan. The district auditor then wrote saying that in his provisional view the establishment of a company and the giving of a loan guarantee was outside council's powers. Credit Suisse sued the council.

Rejecting the claim at first instance, Coleman J saw no reason in principle why a council could not set up a company by using its existing 'incidental' powers under section 111 Local Government Act 1972, which gives a local authority power to do *'anything (whether or not involving the expenditure borrowing or lending of money or the acquisition or disposal of any property or rights) which is calculated to facilitate or is conducive or incidental to the discharge of its functions'*. However, Coleman J concluded that the arrangement was unlawful for two reasons:

- the purpose of the company was to avoid normal spending and borrowing constraints. Therefore it had to be ultra vires;
- the project itself was ultra vires as it is no part of a council's function to develop and sell timeshare accommodation.

On appeal ([1997] QB 306), the Court of the Appeal unanimously upheld Coleman J's decision that's the company and the loan guarantee were ultra vires. Delivering judgment, Neill LJ said:

The implied powers in section 111 did not provide an escape route from the statutory controls. That was clear not only as a matter of principle but also so on the construction of section 111 itself. Section 111(3) ensured that the powers exercisable under section 111 had to be used in conformity with the other statutory provisions.

Accordingly the Bank's argument on statutory powers failed at each stage. The establishment of the company and the giving of the guarantee were part of an ingenious scheme designed to circumvent the no doubt irksome controls imposed by central government. The council however could only do what it was empowered to do by statute. Neither the establishment of a company nor the giving of a guarantee fell within its express or implied powers. In the light of that conclusion it followed that the establishment of the company and the giving of the guarantee well ultra vires acts.

On the same date and for the same reasons the same Court of Appeal also rejected Credit Suisse's claim against the London Borough of Waltham Forest, which had involved a £9 million loan guarantee. In that case the Appeal Court reversed an earlier decision by Gatehouse J *(Credit Suisse v Waltham Forest LBC –* (1994) *Times,* 2 November), when he had upheld both the formation of a company and giving of a loan guarantee.

In the *Waltham Forest* case, the council had formed a joint venture company with a private sector partner which specialised in housing financing and leasing. The new company would buy houses on mortgage and lease them to the council on short-term tenancies. Waltham Forest would pay a full market rent for each of the new properties, for which it would qualify for a housing subsidy. At the end of the lease period, the houses would be sold and the proceeds used to pay off the loan. Unfortunately, tumbling property prices meant that when the properties were eventually sold, the proceeds were insufficient to clear the debt.

Gatehouse J had said at first instance that the council had a duty to accommodate homeless people and power to buy houses for that purpose. In this case the council had acquired the houses by leasing them from the company, which it could not have done without giving a loan guarantee. Therefore, the giving of the guarantee was conducive to the discharge of the council's homeless duties and within section 111. The Court of Appeal disagreed and ruled that the arrangement was ultra vires:

> *Section 101 [Local Government Act 1972] contained detailed provisions relating to what arrangements could be made for the discharge of functions by local authorities. These powers were very limited and did not entitle a local housing authority to discharge any of their functions by means of a partly owned company. Could that power or the power to give such a company assistance in the form of a guarantee or indemnity be implied by reason of Section 111?*

The Court of Appeal calculated that where Parliament had made detailed provisions as to how certain statutory functions were to be carried out, there was no scope for implying the existence of additional powers which are wholly outside the statutory code.

That it was possible for a local authority to set up or participate in a company had previously been recognised in Part V Local Government and Housing Act 1989 (LGHA), which set up a statutory framework for the future regulation of local authority companies (including industrial and provident societies), though the LGHA did not give local authorities any new powers to set up companies or even clarify those powers (if any) which already existed. The LGHA classes local authority companies as: controlled; influenced; arm's length; or minority interest companies.

A company is deemed to be 'controlled' by a local authority if, within company legislation, it is a subsidiary of that local authority; or if it not strictly a subsidiary but the local authority has the right to appoint or remove a majority of the directors; or it is under the control of another company which is itself under local authority control. A local authority-controlled company can also be deemed to be 'arm's length' for any financial year if before the beginning of that financial year the local authority passed a resolution that the company should be 'arm's length' and, since the passing of that resolution, each director has been appointed for a term of at least two years and (unless the Secretary of State has otherwise directed) no director has been removed by members' resolution.

The company is deemed by the LGHA to be 'influenced' by a local authority if it is neither a controlled company nor associated with banking or insurance; at least 20% of total voting rights are held by persons associated with the local authority or at least 20% of directors are so associated, or at least 20% of the total voting rights at a directors' meeting are held by associated persons; (and in all cases) that there is a 'business relationship' between the company and the local authority. Such a business relationship is deemed to exist in any of the following circumstances:

- Within a 12-month period the aggregate of payments to the company by the authority or by another controlled company represents more than one half of the company's turnover as shown in its profit and loss account.
- More than half of the company's turnover is derived from the exploitation of assets in which the local authority or other controlled company has any interest (disregarding a land interest which is subject of a lease granted for more than seven years).
- The aggregate of local authority capital grants or loans (made or guaranteed by the local authority) exceeds one half of the current or fixed assets of the company.
- The company at any time occupies property which it obtained from a legal authority (or another controlled company) at less than the best consideration reasonably obtainable.

Companies other than 'controlled' or 'influenced' companies in which a local authority has an interest can be referred to as 'minority interest' companies. Section 71(2) LGHA prohibits a local authority from buying shares, becoming a member, nominating members or directors, or permitting a council officer to make any nomination or appointment unless that company is an authorised company for the purposes of section (1)(b) of that Act. This is not as restrictive as first appears as article 11 Local Authorities (Companies) Order 1995 (LACO) defines as 'authorised' any company (other than one regulated under that Order) in which anyone associated with a local authority has a right to vote at general meeting or is a director.

Section 70 LGHA allows the Secretary of State to make regulations relating to local authority controlled or influenced companies. The sanction for non-compliance with those regulations is that any payment made to the company, otherwise incurred contrary to regulations, is deemed to be unlawful expenditure for the purposes of the Audit Commission Act 1998. It is pursuant to section 70 that LACO was made. Under LACO the main distinction is not between controlled, influenced or minority interest companies, but between public sector-led companies which are regulated and private sector-led companies which are not regulated. Article 1(4) LACO defines a local authority company to be regulated if it is *either* a controlled company *or* it is influenced company and satisfies one of the following two tests:

- Test 1: the authority would, if it were itself a limited company, be treated under company law as having the right to exercise a 'dominant influence' over the company in question.
- Test 2: if the authority were a registered company, it would be required under applicable accounting standards, to prepare group accounts for the company in question.

It will be seen that whilst local authority control or influence is a precondition of regulation under LACO, an influenced company limited by shares will only be regulated if it passes either Test 1 or Test 2 above. Influenced share capital companies which pass neither of these tests will be in the same position as any other unregulated minority interest company. In addition to the legal requirements which apply to every company, the provisions relating to regulated companies:

- require that it mention on relevant documents the fact that it is a company controlled or as the case may be influenced by a local authority within Part V LGHA, and naming the relevant authority or authorities. 'Relevant documents' mean business letters, notices and certain other company documents;
- restrict the amount of expenses payable to the director of a regulated company to what would be payable in respect of a comparable duty carried out by that person on behalf of the local authority;
- prevent the company from publishing any material which the local authority would be prohibited from publishing under section 2 Local Government Act 1986 (material designed to affect public support for a political party);
- require company resolutions removing any directors becoming disqualified from membership of a local authority, save where such disqualification has resulted only as a result of their employment with a local authority;
- require the company to provide such information as the local authority appointed auditor may require to carry out their statutory functions;

- require a regulated company to provide to any member of a local authority such information about the affairs of the company as that member requires to carry out their democratic functions;
- require a regulated company, on the request of any relevant authority, to provide to that authority such information about the affairs of the company as that authority may require for the purposes of an order for the time being in force under section 39 (revenue accounts and capital finance) LGHA;
- require a controlled company to obtain the Audit Commission's consent for the appointment of its auditor;
- require a controlled company (which is not an arm's length company) to make its minutes available for inspection by any member of the public (save to the extent that any such disclosure would contravene any enactment or obligation owed to any person).

The regulations regarding capital finance and liabilities as regards any regulated company are all dealt with in articles 12–17 LACO. Each local authority and its associated regulated companies are defined as a 'local authority group', and things done by or to a regulated company all treated as if they were done by or to the local authority itself.

What was particularly notable about the *Allerdale* and *Waltham Forest* judgments was that both councils successfully argued their own ultra vires to avoid payment of a loan, which a finance institution had previously entered into in good faith. The net result was a loss of confidence amongst private sector investors when dealing with local authorities because of the risk that their contracts would be ruled ultra vires. Without such investor confidence the private finance initiative, which had become a preferred option for the delivery of major projects, could not be viable. It was to restore such investor confidence that one of the first legislative acts of the incoming Blair Government was to pass the Local Government (Contracts) Act 1997. The essence of that legislation is that:

- every statutory provision conferring or imposing a function on a local authority also confers power on that local authority to contract with another party to provide or make available assets or services (with or without goods) for the purposes of or in connection with the discharge of that function by the local authority;
- where a local authority enters into a contract, that contract shall (if certified in accordance with the provisions of the Act) be deemed to be within the powers of the local authority, which have been properly exercised for that purpose. In other words, a local authority can warrant its own vires. The Act then set out the process for certifying a contract.

Since the 1994 Court of Appeal judgments in *Allerdale* and *Waltham Forest*, the law relating to local authority companies has also moved on in other ways and local authorities (and other parties dealing with them) are now less likely to find themselves being adjudged to have acted outside their statutory powers. The changes which have taken place in the intervening years can be summarised as follows:

- County, district and unitary councils (though perhaps not yet towns or parishes) now have express statutory powers to set up companies and to trade. It means that councils are no longer reliant on 'incidental' powers, such as section 111 Local Government Act, to carry out their statutory functions through a separate corporate entity.
- On the date LACO came into force, local authorities had a choice of only the two types of corporate entity: a company (with or without a share capital) or an industrial and provident society (which was the corporate structure favoured by many housing associations at that time). Now local authorities and their business partners can structure the corporate activities in many different ways, including new limited liability partnerships and community interest companies.

As what any local authority can do has always been circumscribed by statute, the policy of successive governments (since the Blair years) has been to broaden the statutory powers available to a local authority to include almost anything which has some relevance (whether directly or indirectly) to its statutory functions. An out-of-borough investment acquisition may have no direct link to the carrying out of an in-borough statutory function, save in so far as the profits from that investment acquisition can be ploughed back into the delivery of public services. The idea of a local authority building houses for outright sale might at one time have been considered as ultra vires as it is no part of a recognised delivery function to act as a commercial housebuilder. However direct local authority involvement in schemes to deliver new homes for outright sale are now a mainstream route to cross-subsidise the development of social housing for rent or shared ownership. It begs the question as to whether *Allerdale* might have been decided differently today: bearing in mind that the underlying purpose of that ill-fated scheme was to provide income or capital profits which could be ploughed back into public services. We can be even more confident that *Waltham Forest* would now be decided differently, because the intention of that scheme was to enable the local authority to address local housing need in the most financially advantageous way possible. It was just unfortunate that this happened to coincide with the bottom falling out of the housing market. But if the scheme had succeeded, would it have ever become newsworthy?

It was the (since repealed) section 2 of the Local Government Act 2000 which (under the heading 'Promotion of well-being') gave every local authority power to do anything which they considered likely to promote or improve the economic, social or environmental well-being of their area. It included power to: incur expenditure; give financial assistance; enter into arrangements or agreements; co-operate with or facilitate or co-ordinate the activities of any person; exercise on behalf of any person any functions of that person; or to provide staff, goods, services or accommodation to any person. However, section 3 made clear that this general power took subject to any statutory limitations contained in other legislation and enabled the Secretary of State to make regulations limiting the exercise of this power or to issue statutory guidance to which local authorities were obliged to have regard. Section 4 of that Act also required every local authority to prepare a 'sustainable community strategy' for promoting or improving the economic, social or environmental well-being of their area and contributing to the achievement of sustainable development in the UK.

Section 95 Local Government Act 2003 under the heading 'Power to trade in function related activities through a company' (which currently remains in force), gave the Secretary of State power to make regulations enabling principal councils to do for a commercial purpose anything which they are authorised to do for the purpose of carrying out any of their ordinary functions. The main statutory proviso is that local authorities cannot undertake commercial activities directly but only through a limited company in which the local authority has an interest. Several ministerial orders have been made pursuant to section 95, the most recent being the Local Government (Best Value Authorities) (Power to Trade) (England) Order 2009 (SI 2009/2393) which came into force 1st October 2009 and applies to all 'best value' local authorities. It is only three paragraphs long, the operative paragraph being **Article 2**, which states:

> *(1) subject to paragraphs (2) and (3), a best value authority is authorised to do for a commercial purpose anything which it is authorised to do for the purpose of carrying out any of its ordinary functions.*
>
> *(2) Before exercising the power conferred by paragraph (1), the authority shall-*
>
> > *(a) prepare a business case in support of the proposed exercise of that power; and*
> > *(b) approve that business case.*
>
> *(3) a best value of authority shall recover the costs of any accommodation, good, services, staff or any other thing that it supplies*

116 Local authority companies

to a company in pursuance of any agreement or arrangement to facilitate the exercise of the power conferred by paragraph (1).

Article 2 of the 2009 Ministerial Order describes a 'business case' as comprising a comprehensive statement as to: the objectives of the business; the investment and other resources required to achieve those objectives; the risks the business might face and how significant those risks are; and the expected financial results of the business, together with any other relevant outcomes that the business is expected to achieve. In other words, what is required is a sound commercial business plan before the company starts trading. The key requirement for any local authority trading company set up under section 95 is that its proposed activities will be 'function related'. It means that the local authority must be empowered to provide those goods and services in relation to a statutory function but is not under any obligation to do so. A local housing company set up to develop housing new-build (both for sale or rent) could be said to be 'function related' because it relates to a council's statutory responsibilities to address housing need its area.

Although section 95 and the 2009 Ministerial Order remain technically in force, most local authorities setting up companies and entering into new commercial arrangements now prefer to rely on the wider powers conferred by Part 1 Chapter 1 of the Localism Act 2011. Section 1(1) of that Act states simply that, '*A local authority has power to do anything that individuals generally may do.*' The remaining seven sections of Chapter 1 qualify the scope of that general power, the most relevant being section 4 (Limits on doing things for a commercial purpose in exercise of a general power). Section 4 states:

(1) The general power confers power on a local authority to do things for a commercial purpose only if they are things which the authority may, in exercise of the general power, do otherwise than for a commercial purpose.

(2) Where, in exercise of the general power a local authority does things for a commercial purpose, the authority must do them through a company.

(3) A local authority may not in exercise of the general power do things for a commercial purpose in relation to a person if statutory provision requires the authority to do those things in relation to the person.

(4) In this section 'company' means –

    (a) a company within the meaning giving by section 1(1) Companies Act 2006, or

(b) a society registered or deemed to be registered under the Co-operative and Community Benefits Societies and Credit Unions Act 1965 [now the Co-operative and Community Benefit Societies Act 2014] or the Industrial and Provident Societies Act (Northern Ireland) 1969.

Where Chapter 1 of the 2011 Act is wider than section 95 of the 2003 Act is that it makes no specific reference to the need for the commercial activity being 'function related'. It is instead sufficient that the local authority has 'power' to carry out that activity otherwise that for a commercial purpose. What is also notable is that neither the 2003 nor the 2011 Acts make any reference to a local authority being empowered to trade through a limited liability partnership (as an alternative to a registered company), although it is clear that many local authorities do trade through such corporate entities. In his 9th March 2016 House of Commons briefing paper *The General Power of Competence* Mark Sandiford provides more background information about these new statutory powers and how they should be used.

With the new 'General Power of Competence' it is tempting to think that councils really can do anything. But the reality is that, however widely legislation is drawn, a general power of competence is never absolute, for which there will always be timely judicial reminders.

In *R (ex parte Risk Management Partners) v Brent LBC* [2008] EWHC 692 (Admin), the issue was whether a group of London boroughs could use the 'well-being' power to establish the London Authorities Mutual Limited, a mutual insurance company, to reduce insurance costs. Risk Management Partners, a potential alternative insurance provider, successfully obtained a judicial review decision to the effect that councils could not use the well-being power to enter into this type of arrangement. It was then left to Parliament to plug the gap with sections 34–35 of the Local Democracy, Economic Development and Construction Act 2009, to give local authorities specific powers to establish mutual insurance companies.

The core function of a local authority is to provide public services. Everything else is 'incidental' and open to potential challenge if it strays too far from that core function. The new general power of competence does not override the general principles of public law (as originally laid down in *Associated Provincial Picture Houses v Wednesbury Corporation* [1948] 1 KB 223), which continue to govern legal authority decision making. In paragraph 3.5 of his 2016 briefing paper, Sandiford flags up the following concern expressed by central government:

The government is aware that some authorities are using the general power of competence under the Localism Act 2011 to develop new social or affordable housing and accounting for that stock in its General Fund. Accounting for stock in this way is not in line with Government policy and if councils continue to develop social or affordable stock which they fail to account for within the Housing Revenue Account the Secretary of State will consider issuing a direction under section 74 of the Local Government and Housing Act 1989 to bring the stock into the Housing Revenue Account.

While the Localism Act 2011 recognises only registered companies and what were formerly known as industrial and provident societies (now known under the Co-operative and Community Benefit Societies Act 2014 as 'registered societies') there are other corporate options. One such alternative is the limited liability partnership (or LLP) which is registered under the Limited Liability Partnership Act 2000. LLPs contrast with a traditional partnership, where the liability of individual members to contribute to its debts is unlimited. With an LLP those liabilities are capped is the same way as a limited liability company. But, unlike companies, there is no liability for corporation tax. However, setting up an LLP is not appropriate for an organisation which is wholly owned by a local authority. The clue is in the word 'partnership', which means that it provides an optional organisational structure for a special purpose vehicle for a joint venture between a local authority and its private sector partner. Registration as a community benefit society under the Cooperative and Community Benefit Societies Act 2014 provides an alternative corporate limited liability structure under which the organisation is now known simply as a 'registered society'. This type of corporate entity has its origins in the cooperative and building society movements of the 19th century. All that the 2014 Act did was to consolidate that historic legislation and put it all in one place. Because of the need to convince the Financial Conduct Authority that the organisation is set up to provide a community benefit, registered societies take substantially longer to set up than companies, which can be registered instantly online. Even when it is decided to register the organisation as a company under the Companies Act 2006, there are the following alternative options:

- a company with a share capital (which is the norm for most companies which are set up to trade commercially for profit);
- a company limited by guarantee (which is an optional structure for a not-for-profit organisation such as a registered housing provider);
- a community interest company, which is a new type of company established by the Companies (Audit, Investigations and Community Enterprise) Act 2004, as later consolidated into the Companies Act 2006. The approval of the Community Interest Regulator is required when

Local authority companies 119

a community interest company (or CIC) is to be set up. Establishing a CIC requires firstly a community interest statement explaining what the company intends to do. Secondly, there must be an asset-lock, which is a statement that the company's assets will only be used for its social objectives with limits on the amount of money it can pay to shareholders.

A significant consideration when setting up any new corporate entity is to find the organisational structure which is the most tax efficient. One other consequence of a local authority either setting up its own subsidiary organisation, or participating in a joint venture vehicle, is that it adds an extra layer of bureaucratic control. As well as complying with legislation applicable to local authorities, councils, councillors and local government officials who take up membership or directorships of subsidiary companies must also ensure strict compliance with company legislation. A company's constitution is its memorandum and articles of association. Traditionally the 'memorandum' sets out the company objectives whilst the articles of association provide the first point of reference for any procedural issue relating to the way the company or its directors carry on business. Those originating documents must in turn be fully consistent with the requirements of the Companies Act 2006. Particular attention is drawn to sections 171–177 of the Companies Act 2006 which list the general duties which apply to all company directors (and which in many ways are not dissimilar to the duties owed by an elected member to their own local authority). These director duties can be summarised as follows:

- A company director must act in accordance with the company's constitution and only exercise powers for the purposes for which they are conferred.
- A company director must act in good faith and in the way considered most likely to promote the success of the company for the benefit if its members as a whole, having regard amongst other things to: the likely long-term consequences of any decision; the interests of company employees; the need to foster the company's business relationships with suppliers, customers and others; the impact of the company's operations on the community and environment; the desirability of the company maintaining a reputation for high standards of business conduct; and the need to act fairly between members of the company. Where the purposes of the company consist of or include purposes other than the benefit of its members, references to promoting the success of the company refers instead to those other purposes.
- A director of a company must exercise independent judgment.

- A director of a company must exercise such reasonable care, skill and diligence as would be exercised by a reasonably diligent person having the general knowledge, skill and experience reasonably expected of a person carrying out those director functions (having regard also to such general knowledge, skill and experience that the particular director has).
- A director of a company must avoid a situation in which his own personal interests may conflict with the interests of the company: with particular regard to the exploitation of any property, information or opportunity. However, this duty does not apply to a conflict of interest arising from a transaction or arrangement by the director with the company. Neither does it apply if this situation either cannot reasonably be regarded as likely to give rise to a conflict of interest or if the matter has been authorised by the directors.
- A company director must not accept a benefit from a third party conferred by reason of his being a director or his doing (or not doing) anything as a director. However, this duty is not infringed if the acceptance of the benefit could not reasonably be regarded as likely to give rise to a conflict of interest.
- If a director of a company is in any way directly or indirectly interested in a proposed transaction or arrangement with the company, he must declare the nature and extent of that interest to the other directors and such declaration must be made before the company enters into the particular transaction or arrangement.

The fundamental principle of limited liability is that the members and directors of a limited company do not put their own personal assets at risk if the company fails. Their liabilities are limited to the amount of the share capital they have invested in the company or what they are prepared to guarantee (in the case of a company limited by guarantee). But there are some circumstances when a director can be held personally liable for a company's acts or omissions.

Directors can be penalised if the company fails to comply with regulatory requirements involving the late filing of documents. More seriously, they can be held personally liable to creditors for the debts of an insolvent company where it is found either that:

- there has being 'fraudulent trading' within the meaning of section 313 Insolvency Act 1986, where the company has carried on business with intent to defraud; or
- there has been 'wrongful trading' within the meaning of section 314, when the company has continued to trade after it has become obvious that it would not be able to pay its debts.

Local authority companies 121

It is because of such residual risk of personal liability that it is recommended that company directors and other senior company management have in place adequate directors and officers insurance. Unfortunately, a restricted market for such insurance means paying a disproportionately high premium for what in reality is a very remote risk. The alternative is for a local authority to indemnify company directors and officers directly using their powers under the Local Authorities (Indemnities for Members and Officers) Order 2004, the material provisions of which are:

- **Article 4** – which allows a local authority to purchase insurance for its members or officers instead of providing a contractual indemnity;
- **Article 5** – which allows a local authority to provide a contractual indemnity to a member or officer in respect of any act or omission which has either been authorised by the authority or arises from powers conferred or duties placed on that member or officer in consequence of any function being exercised either at the request or with the approval of the local authority, or for the purposes of the authority;
- **Article 6** – which prohibits any indemnity being given for something which constitutes a criminal offence or is the result of fraud or other deliberate wrongdoing or recklessness on the part of that director or officer;
- **Article 7** – which allows a local authority to provide an indemnity to the extent that a member or officer reasonably believed *either* that an action or failure to act was either within the powers of the authority *or* (where that action comprised the issuing of any document containing any statement as to the powers of the authority, or any statement that certain steps have been taken or requirements fulfilled) believed that the contents of that statement were true;
- **Article 8** – which states that the terms of any indemnity given (or insurance secured) shall be such as the authority shall agree, save that the cost of any indemnity or insurance relating to the defence of criminal proceedings or allegations that a member has breached the authority's code of conduct should be reimbursed if that person is finally convicted of that offence or if it is ultimately found that the member has failed to comply with the code of conduct.

Index

allotment 37
appropriation 29–31, 34, 64, 66–68
arm's length company 110
assured shorthold 4

basic loss payment 54
bond issue 94–95

Cabinet Report 11–12, 58–59, 79–82
capital finance 92–93
charging schedule 90
charity land 38
Civitas Report 2–3
common land 38–39
community engagement 12
community infrastructure levy 90–91
compensation 54
conditions precedent 104
confirmation (of CPO) 51
construction 103
contract notice 82
contractual relationship 99–100
controlled company 110
costs 55
cross-subsidisation 92

decree of ineffectiveness 83
deed poll 53
demolition notice (initial and final) 72–75
development agreement 102–106
Development Partner Panel 3 84–85
director (company) 119–120
disturbance payment 54
drainage and water search 20

Electronic Communications Code 70–72
environmental search 20

framework contract 84–85

general consent 24–29, 36–37
general vesting declaration 53–54
grants 96
green belt 39
Grenfell 13–14

highway 38, 75–78
home loss payment 54
housing assistance 60–62
housing benefit 2–3
Housing Revenue Account (HRA) 23
human rights 48–49, 68

incidental powers 109
indemnity agreement (of CPO) 106
influenced company 111–112
insurance (directors and officers) 121–122
invitation to tender 83, 99–100

joint venture 46–47

land referencing 49
land registration 15–19
limited liability partnership 118

minority interest company 112

notice of entry 53
notice to treat 53

objections 51–52
OJEU notice 82
open space 37–38
overage 106

partnering 107
private finance initiative 95
prudential borrowing 92–95
public relations 12
public right 75–78
Public Works Loan Board 94

registered provider 46
resolution 49
right of way 75–78
right-to-buy 5–7
risk 12–14

searches 19–21
secure tenant 4–5, 41

stamp duty land tax 86–88
state aid 96–98
statement of reasons 55–56

tax increment financing scheme (TIF) 94
telecommunications operators 70–72
tender 82–84
title 11
trading (powers) 115–119

UK Municipal Bonds Agency 94–95
unregistered land 16–17
Upper Tribunal (Lands Chamber) 63–64
utilities 69–70

value added tax 88–90
village green 38

warranties (construction) 105